A BOX OF TRINKETS

Stories, Poems, Songs, Musings, Comments and Memories

Allen Johnson, Jr.

PREMIUM PRESS AMERICA
NASHVILLE, TENNESSEE

A Box of Trinkets by Allen Johnson, Jr.

Published by PREMIUM PRESS AMERICA

Copyright © 2002 PREMIUM PRESS AMERICA

All rights reserved. No part of this book may be reproduced or transmitted in any form or by any means, electronic or mechanical, including photocopying, recording, or by any information storage and retrieval system, without prior written permission of the Publisher, except where permitted by law.

ISBN 0-9637733-2-1

Cover and page design by Armour&Armour
Cover photo by Catherine Pittman Smith
Trinkets courtesy of Jim Reed

First Edition 2003

1 2 3 4 5 6 7 8 9 10

For Conrad, Margot, Colby,
April and Ben

ACKNOWLEDGMENTS

Heartfelt thanks to all the friends who have loved and tolerated me and, in the case of this book, encouraged me: Martin DeVore, Brother Hare, Richard Braunlich, Linda Johnson, Ernie Stires, Bob and Jo Lovell, Cynthia Rountree, Father Benjamin Bell; and to my friend, Harry Horse, for his appearance on the cover.

Thanks to my editor, Alison Glascock and to Jim Reed for his foreword and many of the trinkets in the cover photograph.

My special thanks and love go to the one who has helped me the most to grow, my wife, Jill.

This book reflects my life-journey towards becoming a fully eccentric "character." I want to thank to my mother-in-law, Rose Marshall, for showing me the way!

CONTENTS

Foreword	vii
Preface	ix
Froggy Rochelle	1
Ego Trip	5
Maturity	6
Spring of Joy	7
Meeting Hemingway	8
Two Jennys	10
Innocence	11
The Hungry Bird Blues	13
International Criminal	14
Bluebird	15
Lost Potential	16
The Wind in the Willows	18
Everybody Loses	21
Moment of Glory	22
The Bungler	26
Meeting Dr. Einstein	27
The Maple Tree	28
Dogs	29
I Saw a Faceless Man	31
Crawford Johnson and the Early Days of Coca-Cola	32
What Color the Wind?	34
Uncle	35
Letter to a Child	41
The Warp and Woof of God	43
Confession of a Sexist	44
The "TR" Words	46
Snow White and the Seven Dwarfs	47
Reading Novels for Inspiration	48
Howard Spring, Novelist	53
Sexcouplets	54

The Emperor's Blue Clothes	56
I Dream That I Am Bix's Dad	59
A Sixty-Year-Old Boy Remembers Trains	60
My Turtle's in the Toilet	66
Rose	67
To An English Soldier	68
My Other Half	70
The Skeptical Believer	71
The Wrong Duck	76
The Chain of Life	78
Thoughts on Writing *My Brother's Story*	79
Potato Soup Surprise	83
Memories of a Classic Yacht	84
Indigo Buntings	91
Colorado Chic	92
Water	93
My Discovery	94
My Little Painting	97
Let Us Think	98
The First Christmas Eve	100
The Flimflams	102
Three Words	104
Connected Springs?	105
Continuum	109
The Lady in Red	110
Did Jesus Laugh?	118
Opposing Mirrors	120
Bovine Suffrage	121
Fibber McGee and Molly	122
Young Men on Fire!	125
My Winnie the Pooh Tea Mugs	126
Bother and O Blow!	127
Four Extraordinary Women I Never Knew	128
The Apology	130
Romance on I-65	132

FOREWORD

There's nobody quite like Allen Johnson, Jr.

This declaration could be a frightening commentary or a celebratory compliment, but you'll have to decide for yourself.

As you journey through these pages, be prepared to be unprepared for what you experience. Where else would you ever find stories, poems and comments in one volume on: a faceless man, William Jennings Bryan, sexism, high-fashion-macho cowboys, topless dancers? In what other book will you meet in person Albert Einstein, Nat King Cole and Ernest Hemingway, along with assorted dogs, lovers, authors, painters and just plain offbeat but very real people?

Allen's pages are full of potato soup surprises, feisty army sergeants, inventive soldiers, luxury yacht voyages, train rides you wish you had taken yourself and an occasional slap on the wrist for all the silly things society tries to serve up without first being asked.

This is a collection of unapologetic stories and comments written by an unapologetic Southern writer unlike any other writer you've met. Allen Johnson, Jr. grabs you with big ideas, tiny meanderings, timely ideas and slightly irreverent musings. Once you start the journey through these trinkets, you won't want to stop till you get to the bottom of the box.

Pay particular attention to Allen's romantic quest for a wonderful wife and a second chance at life (see "Connected Springs"). That tale alone is worth the price of admission! And be prepared to argue with him. He has opinions that he does not mind sharing: opinions on religion, the mass media, modern art, the good old days in the South, the power of just being yourself.

Read this book with the assurance that Allen will be looking over your shoulder and guiding you through the wildflower words and surprising side-path ideas. You'll know he's there because, as he and I both believe, people can feel your gaze in this world. And since his gaze is kindly and playful, you, too, will exhale with relief, gasp with joy, chuckle here and there and come out to play.
—Jim Reed, author, *Dad's Tweed Coat: Small Wisdoms, Hidden Comforts, Unexpected Joys*

PREFACE

As I enter the final phase of my life, the impulse comes to me to gather up some bits and pieces—fragments that may have color or reflect some spark of light—and see if they will somehow combine into a mosaic. Perhaps a pattern will emerge that will show some meaning that is greater than the sum of the parts. I doubt this, however. What I am doing, I suppose, is tidying up before vacating the premises, putting odds and ends into a collection so that someone—perhaps my descendants—will be able to poke around in these written trinkets, see a sparkle here or some color there and find some continuity with the past. More and more I believe that connectedness with the past—continuity—helps to give meaning to the flow of this amazing experience we call life.

Looking back with pure sentimentality trivializes the past into nostalgia, but there are memories worth preserving and passing down. I can only hope that I have looked back with enough humor and insight to avoid the nostalgia trap.

Other pieces in this collection have to do with my connectedness to people, to nature and to God. It is interesting to me that connectedness gives meaning to this astonishing mystery in which we are immersed.

Some of these bits and pieces satirize or criticize aspects of modern life. As a boy, I loved to shoot my BB guns. These—unless they were pointed at a fragile bird or someone's eye—were more toys than weapons. As a man, I have continued to take potshots—in my writing—at some of the phoniness and bad values that I see in modern life. Unlike many intellectuals, however, I don't believe that my satires or criticisms will have much effect. I feel exactly like I am shooting BBs at tin cans. There still is, however, considerable satisfaction in hitting the can dead center!

As a boy, I was always collecting favorite things in to a box or drawer. A favorite slingshot kept with a silver dollar . . . a special knife . . . a magic trick . . . .

As a man, I haven't changed. This collection is another box of trinkets. Some of these trinkets were written for fun . . . some to make a point . . . some to remember. A few may have some small, artistic value.

Make of them what you will.

FROGGY ROCHELLE

"Get up! Get up! GET UP" Sergeant Rochelle's bass voice ascended the scale. "All right you hoods! Unass dem fart sacks!" It was four-thirty in the morning—basic training at Fort Hood, Texas—and Sergeant Rochelle's wake-up call was greeted with a chorus of groans and a stream of profanity and maniacal laughter from the other end of the barracks as Private James Johnson's feet hit the cold linoleum floor. I thought then, and I still think, that "unass" is one of the more creative verbs I have run across.

Sergeant Rochelle was impressive. With his barrel chest, huge neck, protruding eyes and deep bass voice, he resembled a giant, black bullfrog. When he was not present, we called him "Froggy," and Froggy Rochelle, whose upper arm was as big as my thigh and who could do one-armed pushups, was held in high regard by the men of our platoon in basic training at Fort Hood. He, on the other hand, looked on us with the fond, amused contempt that a giant bullfrog might give to a bunch of tadpoles that might never make the transformation. We had olive green fatigues and combat boots and we were called "private," but we were a long way from being soldiers.

Still, we felt like soldiers. There was an atmosphere about basic training that absorbed you. The Army owned us . . . mind and body. As we stood in formation in the chilly Texas dawn, smoking, spitting, bitching and joking, waiting for someone to march us to the mess hall where we would drink the fragrant, muddy, boiled coffee and eat creamed chipped beef on toast (shit on a shingle), we knew we were no longer civilians. There were the uniforms and the crew cuts, of course, but most of all, there was this atmosphere and the fact that we no longer had to think. Every move we made was controlled by some sergeant. I was surprised to discover how mentally restful this was. It was like being a child again. As long as you did what you were told, your mind was free to enjoy itself.

The men in our platoon came from all different backgrounds.

There was Jimmy Jowers, an immature black guy from the Mississippi cotton fields who had a babyish face and used to make us laugh by putting his towel on in a way that looked like he was in a diaper. There was Little Joe Formica who came from Ohio and who, with his short muscular body, long face and nose and low hairline, resembled an orangutan. (There were four or five tough Italian guys from this area and most of us tried to stay out of their way.) There were two private James Johnsons: one (the morning curser) had been "sentenced" to the Army instead of reform school; the other, a sallow-faced, froglike person, wanted to get out of the Army so badly that he took to eating soap and throwing up blood. There was Dick Iverson, "The Professor," a Harvard graduate whose slight stutter and ready sense of humor made him well-liked and Charlie Hampton, a tall blond guy with curly hair, whose coarse, slangy humor we all appreciated and who had learned sign language from a deaf girl that he had dated. There was "Baby" Griggs, our black squad leader, who couldn't pronounce the "sh" sound and said "sit!" when he was trying to say "shit!" and who did a little jivey strut when he marched. There was Jessie Gomez, a cheerful, chunky little Indian from Nevada. And there was Nino Lancia ("Lance"), one of a group from Steubenville, Ohio—a six-foot-four guy with a hooknose whose relaxed humor and infectious laugh made him very popular. For some reason, Lance took a liking to me and took me under his protection. After that, I never had to worry about the other Italian guys. If you were accepted by one of them, you were accepted by all. There were fifty of us in the platoon, in all shapes, sizes and colors. For the most part, we got on well with each other. We were budding soldiers, and we had a common problem: the Army.

While Froggy Rochelle was revered, the other "noncoms" in our platoon (a sergeants and a corporal) were not well-liked. Sergeant Pharr—a skinny, red-faced man with a large Adam's apple and a whining, redneck voice—used to chew us out repeatedly with the same litany,

"This barracks looks like a Hungarian revolt! If you don't shape it up, shame on ye!"

One day I was trying to organize my footlocker and while peering into it I said in a nasal, whining voice,

"This footlocker looks like a Hungarian revolt! If I don't shape it up, shame on me!"

I looked around to see Sergeant Pharr standing behind me looking redder in the face than ever. I never got another pass.

There was a most unpleasant and angry young noncom, Corporal Callison, who also had a red face and a really bad stutter. Since he treated us so badly, we all laughed when Charlie Hampton developed a wicked parody of the stutter. He had it to perfection. Somehow the corporal found out, and when he was giving us our usual scathing "ass-chewing" about our miserable performance as soldiers, he wound up with: ". . . and I want to t-t-tell yawl something else. I f-f-found out s-s-s-somebody's b-b-been m-m-mockin' my stutter!" I looked at Charlie who was examining the ceiling with studied nonchalance. No one could have looked more innocent, except for the fact that he had turned as red in the face as Corporal Callison! But I am wandering. Back to Sergeant Rochelle.

In the Army, profanity is so common that after a while you no longer hear it. The old saying that no one swears like an Army cook is not the whole story. In the Army, everyone swears. Froggy Rochelle was no exception, but his profanity was more creative than most.

One of the exercises that every basic trainee had to go through was crawling under barbed wire with live machine gun fire cracking inches over your head. The machine gun barrel rested against a horizontal bar so that it could not be depressed. As long as you stayed close to the ground, you were perfectly safe. Froggy explained it like this:

"You hoods keep down low when you crawlin'. If you don't keep low, you be writin' yo' Mamma tonight, Dear Mamma, You can sell the shithouse, cause I done lost my ass!"

My last memory of Froggy Rochelle is of the night after we completed basic training. We were having a G.I. party, scrubbing the red linoleum barracks floors, before going home for Christmas leave. We were all in high spirits and laughing at the antics of Little Joe Formica who was on his knees with a scrub brush in each hand. As he made two-handed circles with the brushes, he would snap his knees together, propelling himself through the suds like a human scrubbing machine. Sergeant Rochelle came in and stood there staring balefully at us. We all started to cheer,

"Yea, Froggy! Yea, Froggy!"

Sergeant Rochelle started to grin in spite of himself. As he turned away, we heard him say,

"Buncha hoods!"

EGO TRIP

Well he got this little lawyer guy
To search the records down.
Sixteen thousand ten square feet
Was the biggest house in town.

Then he got this little architect,
And he bought a piece of land.
"Give me eighteen thousand feet," he said.
"Make it elegant and grand."

With umpteen million dollars
To lavish and to waste,
The planning was straight forward,
With no regard for taste.

There were soaring roofs to nowhere,
Dramatic walls of glass . . .
They spent a bunch on statues
To give the place some class.

There was marble here and marble there
Gold-plated this and that . . .
A shiny gym with shiny toys,
For taking off the fat.

And all the latest gadgets . . .
There was wall-to-wall TV.
The swimming pool came right inside.
Impressive? Yes, sirree!

But his neighbors were disgusted.
Made fun with jokes and such.
And one dry wit said: "It ain't home,
But it certainly is much!"

MATURITY?

It could be argued that maturity is learning how to be yourself. If this is true, maybe it explains what I was doing yo-yoing in the supermarket when I was fifty-two years old. I have always enjoyed yo-yoing, and supermarkets are boring. . . . Anyway, my wife and I were living in Florida at the time and, like most people, that day in the supermarket, I had on shorts. Well, the yo-yo string broke and the spinning yo-yo went zipping down the aisle with me in hot pursuit. My wife said I was quite a sight bending over in my shorts chasing the escaping yo-yo. My wife is quite a bit younger in years. I think that watching my performance in the supermarket convinced her that I was not as old mentally as I was in years. I prefer to call it maturity!

SPRING OF JOY

It gushes forth,
Bubbling,
Sparkling,
Deep and pure,
Reflecting joy . . .
My little boy's laugh.

MEETING HEMINGWAY

When I was a young man, I became intensely bored with drinking beer in a fraternity at the University of Alabama. I wanted to quit school for a while and work. Thinking, perhaps, that I would be more stimulated in a cosmopolitan setting, my misguided but well-intended parents talked me into going to the University of Geneva in Switzerland. (Due to lack of maturity and the fact that my French was bad, my time at the University of Geneva was not a success, but that is another story.) I was shipped out first class on the *Isle de France*.

There was a hometown socialite and big wheel in the Democratic Party on the boat whom I will call "Dorothy." She had spotted me on the passenger list as someone else from Birmingham. She tracked me down and introduced herself to me. We chatted together for several minutes, and she asked me what I wanted to do when I got out of college. I told her I thought I wanted to be a writer. I forgot about Dorothy after this and proceeded to enjoy myself.

One of the fun things about that crossing was the fact that Ernest Hemingway was on board. He was traveling with his wife, Mary, and several of his friends. There was a small bar that overlooked the bow of the boat where Hemingway used to sit in the afternoons drinking with his friends. I started going to this bar where I would nurse a beer and eavesdrop. I have never liked to bother celebrities and I didn't intrude. I just listened to the stories he was telling his friends. One afternoon, when I was enjoying this harmless eavesdropping, I looked up to see Dorothy approaching the bar. She came right up and started talking to Hemingway, whom she evidently knew. For some reason, I had an intuition that I was in trouble. Sure enough, she said,

"Oooo, Papa, I want you to meet a nice young man who

wants to be a writer." Hemingway shook my hand and turned to his friends and said in a gravelly falsetto,

"Boys, 'I want you to meet a nice young man who wants to be a writer.'" I was looking around for something to crawl under.

Later that afternoon I was sitting in the lounge when Hemingway walked by. He grinned at me and whacked me on the back. I felt he was telling me that he had been making fun of Dorothy and not me. It made me feel a whole lot better. I have always appreciated the fact that he made that gesture.

TWO JENNYS

Cornwall, England

Jenny's ma was poking up the fire,
When the door flew open, and the flames leapt higher.
Jenny came in. She was tall and fair,
With a bloom in her cheek and mist in her hair.
She had picked wild thyme on the cliffs by the sea . . .
Her ma said, "Jen! You're in time for tea."
So they both sat down for a fine old chat,
While the coal fire purred like the old gray cat.
Jenny warmed her toes 'til her boots gave steam,
And they ate blackberries and Cornish cream.

California, U.S.A.

"Jennifer! Jennifer!
I'm off to play bridge.
There's some of that pizza
In the back of the fridge.
I left Suzie's number
By the phone in the hall . . ."
"Don't sweat it, Mom,
I'm going to the mall."

INNOCENCE

Like so many aspects of life, innocence is a mystery. Our little boy is a beautiful example of innocence. It is our job to protect his innocence. One way we try to do this is by not having television. This limits his exposure to pop culture.

I believe pop culture is corrupting the innocence of our children. I rarely watch television or read newspapers or magazines, but whenever I do get a glimpse of pop culture, I am always amazed at how degenerate it is.

Pop culture seems to revolve around celebrities doing bizarre, immoral things. I don't even know who most of these people are. They bore me so much that I can't be bothered to read about them. All I know is that they seem to have no morals, make a lot of money, relish public attention and dress with very bad taste, but I sense that they have a powerful effect on our young people.

The only medium I am exposed to is radio. I have to do a good bit of driving and sometimes listen to public radio but not the news. Why should I listen to some announcer tell me in measured, dignified tones of every horror that goes on all over the world? The current stories are often about bombs killing innocent people in Ireland or Jerusalem. Aren't these the same horror stories that have been in the news for the past ten or fifteen years? I see no reason why I should burden my mind with the repetitive horrors of the world that I am powerless to prevent or mitigate.

To be fair, I must admit that once in a while, public radio gives me a winner. When it does, it is usually music. Yesterday, on public radio, I heard a 1934 recording of Art Tatum playing "Liza." It took my breath away!

I wonder about talk shows. There is a lady psychologist who puts on the radio trashy problems about people's "private" lives and then moralizes about them. I doubt if this lady is really raising the morality of society by dragging all this garbage onto the public airwaves. Isn't she really exploiting the public's insatiable appetite for trash?

Why do people want to air their dirty linen in public, anyway? ("Doctor I have a moral dilemma. I'm sleeping with Jane, but I'm married to Emma!") I suspect that most are motivated by a juvenile need for attention.

Anyway, even minimal exposure to the media convinces me that most pop culture is in bad taste, and much of it is corrupt in the sense that it exploits sex and violence in the youth market. You don't have to know much about pop culture to see how it could harm the innocence of children who are exposed to it.

Even though we have no television, our little boy inevitably became aware of the impeachment that was going on. He asked his half sister, who had been visiting for Christmas, if she thought the president should be impeached. She said, "He's already been impeached."

"Well, if he told a lie," our little boy said, "they should make him go home and go right to his room!"

My little boy's innocence seems perfectly natural, but innocence in adults is a mystery to me. Why do some people retain it and some lose it? Is it possible that some people never had it? What, for example, is the difference in the formation of such opposites as Elisabeth Kubler-Ross and Hitler? Was Hitler evil as a baby? If not, at what point did he change? Why does one person develop into a healer and another into a hurter? Could it be that those who lose their innocence become the hurters? If this is true, why do we tolerate a pop culture that ruins the innocence of children? Do we want to raise a generation of hurters?

I am convinced that innocence is the biggest gift we are given. It is certainly the most precious part of a child—the part most worth protecting.

THE HUNGRY BIRD BLUES

(Written for and about my wife who kept lots of birds in Chelsea, Alabama fat and happy for many years. This is a talking blues "sung" by a mockingbird to a downy woodpecker.)

Down in Alabama out in Chel-sy-ee
Lives a wonderful person called the Bird Lay-dee
I don't know why but it's plain to see,
She loves little birdies like you and me.
Puts out bird food. Every day. Busy little gal.

Well let me tell you how it was I knew.
I heard it from a cardinal who was passing through.
A white-throated sparrow told a chickadee.
He told the cardinal and the cardinal told me.
Birdie grapevine. News travels. 'Specially good news.

So if you want to get full, I can tell you how to do it,
Sunflower seeds, peanut butter and suet . . .
Just get on down to Chel-sy-ee
And check right in with the Bird Lay-dee.
No cats. Birdie heaven. Nothing in your way but squirrels.

Well there's cracked corn laying out on the ground,
Bird feeders hanging up all around.
There's a heated pool that ain't never froze.
You can set right down and soak your toes.
Just sing a little, look purty . . . food keeps a-comin'.

It's a cold, cold winter, but I got good news . . .
There ain't no need to get the hungry bird blues.
Just come on down where the food is free,
From the nice bird lady of Chel-sy-ee.
Good eatin'. Fit for a king. Uh Huh!

INTERNATIONAL CRIMINAL

It is my belief that many black people have the ability to extract the maximum amount of fun out of a situation. Sometimes I am fairly good at it myself.

I was making a minor purchase in an electronics store and, probably to glean marketing data, the young, black sales girl asked me for my phone number.

"I couldn't give out my phone number," I told her.

"Why not?" she asked.

"I'm an international criminal," I said. She pulled her head down on her shoulders, and her eyebrows shot up.

"You what?" she said.

"An international criminal," I said. "If I start giving out my phone number almost anybody will be able to track me down, the police . . . the FBI . . . anybody."

She looked at me, not knowing whether to grin or not, then she looked out at my car which I had parked in front of the store. My little boy's car seat was in the back.

"Uh huh!" she said. "International criminal with a baby seat in the car!"

"Listen," I grinned at her. "If we didn't have babies, the whole criminal class would die out."

When I left, she was laughing and shaking her head.

"Mister, you something else!" she said. "You come back anytime, you hear?"

BLUEBIRD

A tiny bit of sky,
Iridescent blue,
The sunrise on his breast
Perched near me then flew!

LOST POTENTIAL

Is there anything sadder than lost potential?
My father was a natural musician. He was taught how to play by his family's black butler. He flunked out of the Lawrenceville School because he played the piano more than he studied. Then he flunked out of Yale the same way. Before he did, however, he played rhythm piano in a college dance band that was led by Sleepy Hall, considered by many to have been the greatest plectrum banjoist who ever lived. After college, Sleepy took a band to Paris where he was a raging success until the banjo went out of vogue. My dad had wanted to join Sleepy and play professionally and Sleepy had wanted my dad in his band. Dad's father forbade this, however, and insisted that Dad enter the family Coca-Cola bottling business. It was the tail end of the Victorian era, when parental edicts still had force, and Dad's personality was not as strong as his talent. He capitulated.

I always wished that Dad had taken the chance to play professionally. What would have happened is purely hypothetical. His life would have been different. He might not have married my mother. I might not be here. It is useless to ruminate on what might have been, but I do have the feeling that he should have taken a shot at fulfilling his talent. Sleepy wound up as the Postmaster in Butte, Montana, and Dad would probably have wound up back in the family business, but a couple of years as a musician would have been an experience he would never have forgotten.

My dad's playing sparkled with drive, energy and fun. He loved to play for people. He never practiced, but somehow, when he sat down to play, the room would come alive.

When my sister was seventeen and I was thirteen, our parents took us to Europe. One night in Paris they took us to Maxim's where we sat at a table next to the Duke and Duchess of Windsor. At one point, Mother and Dad got up to dance. I heard the Duchess say in her phony British accent,

"Fawncy thet, the parents dawnce and leave the kiddies sitting alone at the table." From her point of view, I am sure it would have been better if the kiddies had been left at the hotel. Anyway, later on Dad went up to the leader of the dance band and asked him if he could sit in at the piano. I don't remember, but I imagine the Duchess was horrified. I wasn't, however. I knew exactly what was going to happen. Half way into the first tune idle chatter stopped. Toes started to tap. The dance floor became crowded. Maxim's, filled with the bored and jaded rich, came alive!

Dad didn't see Sleepy for almost thirty years. For the occasion of Dad's fiftieth birthday party, my mother and my uncle engineered a surprise. They flew Sleepy in for the party and brought him to my uncle's house.

The night of the party was warm and Mother had opened the house up for the party. In the twilight, my uncle slipped Sleepy into the garden where he started to play "Margie," the theme song from the Yale dance band. My dad went completely white.

"My God!" he said, "Sleepy Hall!"

They played until three in the morning.

THE WIND IN THE WILLOWS

When I was a boy, there were no antibiotics and few vaccines. Kids had all the childhood illnesses—measles, mumps, chicken pox—and bad colds or sore throats that could turn into bacterial infections were cause for concern. An outbreak of polio struck terror into parents' hearts. The upshot of all this was that children with careful parents spent a good deal of time in bed.

My mother was too careful. Once, when I was four years old, she found me sharing a lollypop with our golden retriever, Co-Co. I would take a lick . . . then give him a lick. We were taking turns.

Mother ran in the house and called Alf Walker, the family pediatrician. Fortunately, Dr. Walker was down to earth and had a sense of humor.

"Don't worry, honey," he told Mother. "That dog will be just fine!"

During one of my childhood illnesses, my mother introduced me to *The Wind in the Willows*. I am sure my lifelong love of this book has something to do with the fact that Mother read it aloud to me, but there is more to it than that. It is a lovely work and embodies an approach to life that I have always wanted to follow.

I am sure it is odd for a sixty-two-year-old man to identify with a water rat, but Ratty, in *The Wind in the Willows*, is definitely my kindred spirit.

He loves the water. He loves boats. He yearns for adventure but finds himself caught in the coils of responsibility. He writes poems. He has a cozy home and is loyal to his friends.

All my life I have enjoyed boats, the beauty of nature and the warmth of home, hearth and friendship. Nowhere are these aspects of life better portrayed than in *The Wind in the Willows*. I had always wanted to do something associated with this beautiful book, but I had no idea what it could be. I put this dream aside and turned my attention to other interests. Years later, my old dream came back to me all by itself.

For some reason, I wrote a poem called 'Bother and O Blow!' based on Moley in *The Wind in the Willows*. It was a good poem, and I mused to my wife, "I wonder if I could write a series of poems based on *The Wind in the Willows?*" I decided to try. After I had written a few poems, I felt sure I could do it.

"What should I call the collection?" I asked my wife.

"A Breeze in the Willows," my wife answered at once, giving me the perfect title.

My wife is English and we have a small cottage in the little village in Cornwall where she was raised. Our friend and neighbor there, Roger Michelle, is a wonderful potter and graphic artist. He agreed to illustrate my poems. I worked with him all one summer making sure the illustrations and poems suited each other. When the illustrations were finished, what Roger had done was better than I had dared to hope for.

I thought it would be impossible to convince a publisher in the mainstream press to publish a series of poems and illustrations based on a children's book, but—small miracle—we did. Even though the poems are good, I am convinced that Roger Michelle's wonderful illustrations are the reason the book got published.

In the spring of 1998, Ten Speed Press published *A Breeze in the Willows*. The publisher did a superb job designing the book. When the book was printed, much to my pride and joy, I found we had a little gem. I wanted to make a good effort to introduce and promote the release of our book and therein lies another story.

When *A Breeze in the Willows* was published, I sent out advance copies in hopes of reviews. I generated a list of publishers from my old prep school alumni directory. One of these was the publisher of the Little Rock *Democrat Gazette.*

He received the book at home and, not recognizing my name, sent the package to the newspaper to have it "checked out." The paper sent the package to the main post office. By the time the post office got the package, somebody had used the word *bomb.* The bomb squad was called. Soon they had evacuated the post office and cordoned off two blocks around it. The police and firemen were called in. There were nine emergency vehicles. A television news truck arrived. Two men from the bomb squad suited up in body armor snuck up on my little book of poems and blew it up!

A young reporter poked through the remains of the package, found the address label and did what somebody should have done in the first place—he called me up.

After I heard what had happened and had stopped laughing, the reporter said he was writing a front-page story for the paper, and did I know why the "panic button" had been pushed? I said, "Yes" and told him about the following poem:

DANGER! OVERINFLATED TOAD*

Conceited? Yes, he's so puffed up
One fears he may explode.
An ever-present danger when
A toad's too full of Toad!

"Clearly," I told the reporter, "this poem is the reason the bomb squad was called out!"

---

*Reprinted with permission from *A Breeze in the Willows* by Allen Johnson, Jr. Copyright 1997 by Allen Johnson, Jr., Ten Speed Press, Berkeley, CA. Available from your local bookseller, by calling 800-841-2665, or by visiting www.tenspeed.com

EVERYBODY LOSES

I saw a psychological experiment on television.
    A white-coated man watched a white-coated rat swim around in panic in a conical glass beaker. The man had put in water until the rat's hind feet could not quite touch the bottom . . . hence the panic. The man, I thought, has lost more than the rat. I watched . . . and I lost too.

MOMENT OF GLORY

When I was in the Army, I was not what you would call "leadership material." During my two-year career, I rose to the heights of Private First-Class or PFC. The best thing about this was that, as a PFC, it was easier to keep your friends. You didn't have to order them to do stupid things. Those of us who were on the bottom of the chain of command had the common bond of being involved in trying to beat the system. Those of us who made sergeant had to accommodate the system and give stupid orders to their friends. We privates had no power, but we had more fun.

My hitch was in peacetime. It slotted in between Korea and Vietnam, and I found myself stationed in southern Germany—a private in an armored infantry battalion. I became a member of a scout platoon, manning a machine gun in the back of a jeep. There were thirty-three of us including sergeants. With two or three men to a jeep, we had maybe a dozen jeeps. Except for the mortar platoon, we were the only group in the thousand-man battalion who had jeeps—the rest were transported in trucks or armored personnel carriers. This meant that we were often selected for interesting duties that required mobility. We did everything from guarding Army payrolls to playing the "aggressor" in maneuvers with the Green Berets. Such duties involved us in living "in the field" in pup tents and sleeping bags. Peacetime field duty was like one long camping trip. It was far superior to "garrison duty," which subjected you to continual petty, military harassments such as polishing equipment that was already clean, parades and inspections . . . harassments that were collectively known as "chicken shit."

Once in a while the battalion was moved to a training area near the Czech border for maneuvers. On one of these maneuvers,

Tony Torchia and I were selected to look after the coke-burning boiler in the back of the officer quarters—a concrete-block building where the officers slept. Our cushy job was to clean out the ashes during the daytime, stoke up the boiler and see that the officers had hot water, for showers at five in the morning when they got up.

There was a procedure for assuring the early-morning hot water: The firebox had to be stoked before going to bed. The bottom door that controlled the air to the fire had to be closed so that the fire just simmered all night, and the top door had to be left partly open to prevent too much heat from building up. At four-thirty in the morning one of us had to get up, get dressed and trudge over through the wet snow to open the bottom door—which got the draft going—and close the top door to retain the heat. Doing these two small jobs promptly at four-thirty assured the officers of plenty of hot water at five.

There is no one more inherently lazy than a private in the Army. Like dogs, soldiers sleep to help pass the time. Given a ten-minute break, the average soldier can go sound asleep lying on rocky ground with his helmet for a pillow.

After about a week of taking turns getting up in the cold, snowy darkness to open one small, metal door and close another one, I—motivated by basic laziness—suggested to Tony that we automate the process. Tony thought I was nuts but reluctantly came along to the boiler room to see what I had in mind. I had brought along my old-fashioned alarm clock. When it went off, the winding stem on the back of the clock rotated until the alarm bell ran down. I also had found some string. Everything else we improvised in the boiler room.

Here's how it worked: I found a heavy rock, about the size of a grapefruit and tied some string securely around it. I was then able to attach a fifteen-foot length of string to the rock. I then found a sixteen-inch, flat piece of wood that I rested on a windowsill about five feet off the floor. I put the rock on the flat piece of wood so that about a foot of the board stuck out from the edge of the windowsill. The weight of the rock held it in place. There was an old wooden bench along the wall under the window, and I lashed the alarm clock tightly to this bench with more string. I tied a string around the alarm winder of the clock and attached this string to the end of the board that was sticking out from the windowsill. We then found an old piece of scrap metal. It was thin—about two inches wide and eighteen inches long. I was able to bend it into a U-shape. We used the metal "U" to hold the upper boiler door open about four inches and leaned a six-foot-long, heavy iron poker against the door. The weight of the poker held the "U" in place. There was a handy piece of metal with a loop on the end of it extending down from the ceiling. We took the end of the fifteen-foot piece of string that was tied to the rock, threaded it through this loop, passed it down through the 'U' and tied it to the handle of the closed bottom door that controlled the draft. All was ready. I set the alarm to go off in two minutes and we waited. Tony was shaking his head and grinning.

Ring! Crash! Boing! Scrape! Bang! Tinkle tinkle!

The alarm stem wound up the string to the board pulling it down and tipping the rock off the windowsill. When the rock fell it brought tension on the string, which popped the metal 'U' out of the open upper door, and the weight of the poker slid the door shut. The weight of the rock then pulled the bottom door open. Mission accomplished!

Captain Wilby, our Company Commander, happened to be passing by the boiler room and heard the racket. He stuck his head in.

"Johnson, what in the hell is that?" he asked me. I explained the contraption to him and what it did.

"Does it work?" he wanted to know.

"Yes sir," I assured him.

"Let me see it," he ordered.

We rigged it up again.

"Ring! Crash! Boing! Scrape! Bang! Tinkle tinkle!"

Top door shut . . . bottom door open!

"Well, I'll be goddammed!" He swore shaking his head. He went to the door and called the battalion Executive Officer.

"Major Miller! Come here a minute. You got to see this!"

We ran it again for the major.

"Son of a bitch!" he said. "That's the damnedest thing I ever saw!" He stuck his head out the door and called to the Battalion Commander.

"Colonel Johnston! Sir, you've got to see this."

So there we stood in the boiler room . . . two privates surrounded by the battalion's top brass. We explained the setup to the Colonel, rigged it up again, and held our breath for the command performance.

"Ring! Crash! Boing! Scrape! Bang! Tinkle tinkle!" Perfection!

"My god!" said the Colonel. "Rube Goldberg!"

Well, that was our moment of glory, but the glory wasn't the best part. The best part was that I never got up at four-thirty again. Tony didn't trust the invention at first and got up for several mornings to check on it. It always worked. Finally, he said, "To hell with it. I'm not getting up any more."

Every morning after that, we stayed in our warm sleeping bags on our canvas cots sleeping the sleep of the pure at heart and the deeply, inherently lazy.

THE BUNGLER

"Damn!"
The magician curses,
"This bloody saw!"
Opening his box . . .
Discarding her above the waist . . .
He helps the bottom half to stand.
She does a little step or two
Crossing ankles, pointing toes and posing legs.
She minces over to the chorus line
Joining the nameless, faceless ranks . . .
Of topless dancers.

MEETING DR. EINSTEIN

I went to the Lawrenceville School in New Jersey. It was five miles from Princeton, which happened to be the home of Dr. Albert Einstein.

In the '50s, there were no girls at Lawrenceville, and, since we almost never got out of school except for vacations, we would not lay eyes on a girl for months at a time.

Near the end of the long, winter term of my senior year, there was a concert being given at Princeton. Seniors—called "fifth formers" at Lawrenceville—were offered the chance to go to this concert. It was a rare opportunity to get out of school for an evening and I jumped at it.

When the usher was taking me to my seat he said, "You're next to the great man."

"What do you mean?" I asked him.

"Dr. Einstein," he said. I looked and saw the unmistakable profile and halo of white hair of Dr. Albert Einstein.

When I sat down to the left of Dr. Einstein, he was busy speaking to his wife who was seated on his right. They were speaking German. I soon forgot the Einsteins, however, because, as the members of the orchestra took their places on the stage, I saw that one of the violinists was a stunning young woman with long, shining, chestnut hair, a good figure and tender, perfect red lips. Not having seen a girl for two months, I sat there lost in lustful, yearning admiration. For some reason I glanced to my right at Dr. Einstein. He was smiling with a twinkle in his eye.

"Nice, these modern symphony orchestras, ya?" he said in a thick German accent.

"Oh . . . Yes sir!" I replied. "Yes sir!"

I have always loved the fact that such a great man took a moment to understand and establish a common bond with a girl-starved teenaged boy!

THE MAPLE TREE

The maple tree rises behind the wall
A thundercloud of green,
Mysterious in its shadowed inner depths,
Marrying the earth and sky.

DOGS

One could do a lot worse than to try to be like a dog. After all, dogs are morally superior to us.

Of course there are bad dogs—dogs that have been bred or trained to be mean or even vicious—but, on the whole, dogs are good. Unlike a horse, you can trust a dog. It is possible to groom a horse for hours and then walk behind him and he will kick you into the afterlife. A dog, on the other hand, won't betray you. They are consistently kind, trustworthy, loving, forgiving, loyal and fun. Very few of us measure up to them. How do dogs manage to be so good? I think I know. They shake off the bad stuff.

Dogs can move in a way that causes their skin to shake. They shake off water, sleep and emotion. If you spank a dog, immediately afterwards, he will shake off the spanking. If a dog gets cross with another dog, he will shake it off. If you scold or frighten a dog, he will shake it off. Don't try to learn to do this. It just makes you look silly. My wife caught me trying to shake like a dog the other day and gave me a most peculiar look. I should say, she gave me a look that implied that I was most peculiar! I believe, however, that if humans could shake off bad stuff like dogs do, psychotherapists would be out of business.

There is the popular idea that dogs smell bad. Sometimes they do. They are prone to ear mites, impacted anal glands and rolling in carrion—charming little attributes that make you wish that you were a cat lover except that disgusting dog-smells tend to be localized whereas a cat can make the whole house smell bad.

Ah, but did you ever hug a big outdoors dog . . . stick your face in his long winter coat and inhale? You will smell the whole outdoors . . . dried grasses and leaves, the cold winter air, a hint of evergreens from the woods. It is a grounding smell that instantly makes me want to be a boy again roaming the woods with my slingshot and a canine friend scouting ahead with his nose. And the pads of dog paws have a wonderful, pungent, earthy smell. Check it out, but don't let your wife see you smelling your dog's paws—especially if she has just caught you trying to shake!

My Springer spaniel is thrilled when I howl with her. It takes her a while to get into it, but she thinks it's great fun. My wife accepts our howling together as normal. I wonder if she's getting a bit odd.

I SAW A FACELESS MAN

I saw a faceless man
Whose features had been wiped away
By some calamity.
A blank expanse of scar and grafted skin . . .
An orifice from which he still could speak . . .
And though my eyes would not confront
This devastated face,
I heard the man speak simple words of warmth
To put me more at ease.
Then I knew that he was there . . .
Whole . . .
Like you . . .
Like me . . .

CRAWFORD JOHNSON AND THE EARLY DAYS OF COCA-COLA

The oldest Coca-Cola bottling franchise in the world is in Chattanooga, Tennessee. In the early nineteen hundreds, it was bought by my paternal grandfather, Crawford Johnson, shortly after he founded the Birmingham Coca-Cola Bottling Company in Birmingham, Alabama.

He started with one wagon drawn by a mule called Bell, a hand pump and one employee. From this modest beginning came Coca-Cola Bottling Company United—a bottling company that holds a number of franchises in the South and employs three thousand people.

In the early nineteen hundreds, my grandfather moved to Birmingham, Alabama and started the Birmingham Coca-Cola Bottling Company. There is a picture of him with ten employees standing in front of the bottling plant. It is a small brick building on a dirt street with the shabbiest looking awning draped disreputably across the front. He is wearing a dark suit with a vest and a derby hat standing with his hands in his pockets looking like he has the world by the tail—which, judging by the way things turned out, he did.

My grandfather understood quality control.

Once the treasurer of the company, Mr. Rice, came to see him with an idea to save money. He felt that if less Coca-Cola syrup was put in each bottle of Coke, the accumulated savings would be substantial. My grandfather said:

"Mr. Rice, we will put exactly an ounce and a half of syrup

in each six-and-a-half ounce bottle of Coke. If we put any less, we will lose our customers. If we put any more, we will lose our ass!" This kind of thinking has prevailed in the Coca-Cola business, which explains why—no matter where you are in the world—a Coca-Cola always tastes like a Coca-Cola.

My grandfather hated watermelon. In the days before Pepsi, watermelon was the principal competitive source of refreshment. It was sold on the street out of stalls. In the summer, when the watermelons ripened, Coca-Cola sales would fall off. Even after products that imitated Coke became competitive, my grandfather always resented watermelon. Incidentally, it is my belief that Pepsi is the best thing that ever happened to Coke. Without a strong competitor, Coca-Cola would not have done nearly as well.

Crawford Johnson was a good employer. He cared about his employees. He never laid people off. He always paid employees when they were sick. He said that when someone was sick was the time they most needed to get paid. His employees got paid vacations before anyone had heard of such a thing. Later on, when labor unions were on the rise, there was very little they could offer his employees that they didn't already have.

I never really knew my grandfather. My dad went in the Army in 1941, when I was six, and we moved away from Birmingham. Before we moved back, my grandfather had died. I have few memories of him.

When I was four or five, I could not pronounce the letter "r." I remember my grandfather getting a kick out of asking me to say "the wed wose wambled wound the wailwoad twacks." I remember a little pink, wicker chair that he and my grandmother had that played *The Nutcracker Suite* when a child sat in it. I remember being amazed to see him put salt and pepper on half a cantaloupe.

I never really knew my paternal grandfather . . . but I have always been proud of him.

WHAT COLOR THE WIND?

A silvery dawn is waking.
A misty, shining breeze
Is trailing skeins of silver light
That kiss the dreaming trees.

A summer storm is making,
And rumbling down and back
The valley echoes thunder song.
The wind is wet and black.

The sapphire seas are breaking,
The light is shining through.
Against the deep, delighted sky,
The wind is colored blue.

The tender leaves are quaking,
The first that spring has seen.
The breeze is playing games with them.
The wind is colored green.

UNCLE

(Excerpted in part from *FUN! A Boyhood*)

My mother's family followed the Southern custom of giving people affectionate names according to family relationships. Mother's brother, Pascal Shook, Jr., was known as "Brother," her sister, Margaret Gaines, was "Sister" and oddly my grandfather, P. G. Shook, was known as "Uncle." My grandmother was called "Carrie." It was short for Caroline.

While our home was in the woods of a yet-to-be-developed suburb, Uncle and Carrie lived further up Shades Mountain in the country. They were only a mile or two farther out than us, but their way of life was completely different. Our home was designed for modern (1930s) living. Carrie and Uncle's home belonged to the turn-of-the-century, rural South.

My grandfather was a successful businessman and a gentleman farmer. He built their home on a large tract of land on Shades Mountain overlooking Birmingham, Alabama. He had cows—which meant milk, butter, cream and homemade buttermilk—and horses, including a pony named "Eddie Cantor" complete with pony cart. My grandmother, Carrie, had her antiques.

After driving for a mile on a private dirt road that ran alongside the pasture, you would come to my grandparents' weathered, paved drive which climbed past a sweeping, informal lawn to the rambling, ivy-covered sandstone house on the brow of the hill. It was one of those houses that looked like it had grown into the southern countryside. In back of the house, overlooking the valley, was the pavilion, a porch-like structure with a wood-shingled roof, a red linoleum floor, porch furniture, a chain-suspended porch swing and a painted giraffe from a carousel. The pavilion was the scene of family gatherings on long summer evenings.

When we arrived for a family dinner at Carrie and Uncle's, we would usually find Uncle sitting in his tall, upholstered rocker in the small library called "the morning room" listening to the news from the wooden console radio.

Roosevelt horrified my grandfather who was a staunch Republican and conservative businessman. He felt real concern over the socialistic changes of the New Deal. He was interested in factual matters and never read a novel in his life. Once in a while he would take me to a movie. He would watch the newsreel and then sleep through the entire movie. He was a handsome, dignified man who usually wore a vest with his suits and kept a gold watch in his watch pocket with a gold chain across the front of his vest. With his dark eyebrows and contrasting white hair, he was a fine-looking man. So far, I could be describing a stern, Victorian patriarch but, in fact, there was nothing stern about Uncle. He was very affectionate and had the most delightful sense of humor and an irresistible, contagious chuckle.

My grandfather loved to eat and ate like a European, piling up savory combinations of Southern cooking on the back of his fork, which he held in his left hand. Uncle and Carrie had a cook named Maggie Maccadorie—a tiny, bird-like black woman who couldn't have weighed a hundred pounds. Maggie was an artist who, up until about 1940, still cooked on a wood stove. In the tradition of most Southern cooks, vegetables were overcooked with salt pork ("side meat") and meats were well done, seasoned with lots of pepper . . . but somehow—after several homegrown vegetables had appeared, with corn pudding, fried chicken, tomatoes and onions in a vinegar dressing, and homemade biscuits with country butter—your plate would begin to resemble a work of art. Uncle would eat with great gusto and appreciation for a while, and, finally he would pause to make a joke. It was always the same joke, and it was always funny.

"I don't know why it is," he'd say, "but when you eat for about a half hour, you start to lose your appetite!"

I loved the conversation at family get-togethers. I loved my grandfather's stories, Brother's droll comments, Sister's warm, appreciative laugh and Carrie's patient, persistent genealogy. Genealogy was the glue that held these conversations together. Everybody knew everybody and whom everybody was related to. It was all very comforting sitting on the pavilion on a soft summer evening and listening to the grown-ups weave their stories in which everyone was connected.

One of my grandfather's stories is worth recording for posterity. It was a practical joke that fooled a whole town.

My grandfather's father, a pioneer in the steel business in Birmingham, was an executive in the Tennessee Coal and Iron Company (T.C.I.), and T.C.I. had a private railroad car. Uncle talked his father into letting him and a group of his young men friends use the railroad car to travel to the Alabama/Vanderbilt game in Nashville. Spirited young men were known as "gay blades" in those days, and this particular group was certainly spirited.

After leaving Birmingham on the train—and after a few drinks—they discovered that one of them did a pretty good impersonation of William Jennings Bryan, who was a presidential candidate at the time. When the train made a stop, they wired a message to the next town down the line that William Jennings Bryan was going to make an unscheduled stop there and give a short speech. When the train pulled into the next station the whole town was there. They had closed all the stores and even closed the school. The impersonator appeared on the platform at the end of the car in morning coat and top hat and made a well-received campaign speech. Someone got wise. When the train pulled into the next station, there was another crowd waiting. This time, however, the speaker was greeted with eggs and rotten tomatoes that rained down on the private car forcing the speaker to beat a hasty retreat from the platform. Worse than this, when they got to Nashville, the F.B.I. was waiting. Uncle said that what saved them was the fact that before they reached Nashville, the train had gone through a thunderstorm that had washed off most of the disreputable-looking eggs and tomatoes. They were able to give the F.B.I. agents a drink and convince them that it had been a foolish prank that had gotten a bit out of hand. Unhappily, word of the whole thing got back to Uncle's father, Colonel Shook, who was so embarrassed that he became ill and took to his bed for a week. Whenever Uncle told this story, and I heard it a number of times, he would say with considerable emotion that he never forgave himself for upsetting his father so much.

Spending the night at Carrie and Uncle's was always a bit disorienting. Fitting into the way they lived was like slipping gently into the past. Uncle ate a huge breakfast, no lunch, and, after listening to the evening news, a light supper. He retired so early that, in the summer, it wouldn't be dark. This schedule allowed him to be up for his early morning horseback ride and magnificent breakfast before he went to the office.

Although Uncle's company had one of the first air-conditioning dealerships in the state, he didn't believe in it. Their house wasn't air-conditioned. Uncle slept on a sleeping porch—a room on the end of the house that was all windows on three sides. There were two beds and a polished hardwood floor. When I crawled between the clean sheets in the bed next to Uncle's, it seemed unlikely that I would ever get to sleep. With all the windows open to the Alabama twilight, the rhythmic chirring from the cicadas would be frighteningly loud. Then, as I began to dread lying in the dark while Uncle slept, suddenly it would be morning, and I would find myself being boosted up on a huge horse for the morning ride. I didn't ride enough to be good at it, and the horse I was on followed my grandfather's horse, so when I rode with Uncle, it was mainly an exercise in staying on. Thanks to a Western saddle and a saddle horn, I managed.

Breakfast with Uncle was an event. Uncle kept the toaster right on the table in the sunny, little breakfast room that adjoined the kitchen. He always started breakfast with a bowl of cereal garnished with fresh peaches or berries over which was poured cream that was so heavy that it had to be helped out of the pitcher with a spoon. Then Maggie would produce a platter of poached eggs and bacon and a steaming bowl of grits and Uncle would start turning out hot toast two slices at a time. Uncle would spear some poached egg with his fork then cut a bite of toast and spread on some country butter. On top of the egg and toast on the back of his fork would go grits and bacon and then, with obvious pleasure, Uncle would eat the whole elaborate bite. We were blissfully unaware of cholesterol then and Uncle, who lived well into his nineties, must have been immune anyway.

Uncle had a little Dodge coupe with a running board. He kept this car for years but it was always waxed and shiny and never showed any sign of wear. After our lavish breakfast, Uncle would usually drive me home on his way to work. On the long stretch of private dirt road that led to the highway, he would let me ride on the running board. Standing on the outside of the car at twenty-five miles an hour with the fragrant, southern breeze bringing tears to my eyes was as close to flying as I had ever come.

I have other memories of my grandparents and their home: the shaggy, friendly front lawn that swept down from the house and, in the spring, became a sea of jonquils; seeing Carrie, a patrician, white-haired, Victorian lady, hoist the back of her dress to warm the back of her legs by the fire; Uncle singing "The Blue Eagle Jail" ("The Blue Eagle Jail, no jail at all. The bedbugs are crawling all over the walls. Hard times in the Blue Eagle Jail."); the great boulder behind their house that we used to love to climb and play on; the cow path from the barn to the pasture, which was a hidden tunnel through the flowering shrubs; the butter churn on the screened back porch; Carrie's attic room called "the old room," where she displayed her antiques and where the smell and atmosphere of the past were tangible; Uncle sitting with a slingshot on the front porch in the evening shooting pebbles harmlessly at the squirrels to keep them off the bird feeder but really, I suspect, for the fun of seeing them scamper . . . .

All of these memories evoke in me a gentle sense of loss for a way of life that was even then slipping away.

I loved both of my grandparents, but Uncle was and is my ideal. I hope I get to see him again.

LETTER TO A CHILD

Dear Child,
Turn off the television set.
Look somewhere else.
Look inside yourself.
Your dreams are there
Sparkling with adventure.
If your dream-fire sinks, then read . . .
Stories and poems, the fuel of dreams,
Will whisk you back and forth in time and space
And fire the colors of your mind.
Look out.
The world is there.
Forever, the mysterious stars
Roll through velvet heavens.
The sun bakes down on endless summer days.
The thunderclouds pour fire and rain
Into the thirsty earth.
The green of life spills out and out . . .
Your family is there
For loving . . .
For bothering . . .
Your friends are there
For playing . . .
For laughing . . .
For getting into trouble . . .
Naughtiness simmers in your heart.
Let it out!
The long summer evenings wait for you.
Run through the twilight with your friends.
Chase! Hide! Seek! Wrestle! Play!
Fill yourselves with the sweet summer air
Lie in the grass and see the fireflies spark.
Hear the old folks telling tales of days gone by.

A BOX OF TRINKETS

Eat like a wolf.
Fall into sleep too tired to feel
The scrapes and bruises and mosquito bites.
Dear Child,
Turn off the television set.
Look somewhere else . . .
Look in at dreams.
Look out at life . . .
And live!

THE WARP AND WOOF OF GOD

Somewhere I read that one should approach God playfully. This struck me as an original idea, and I resolved to try it some time.

Several months later I was resting, on the edge of dozing off, and I asked a question in my mind, "Hey, God," I thought. "Do you want to come out and play?" My mind was flooded with light and, at the same time, an overwhelming feeling of joy. The light had a woven pattern to it—flat strips of light woven together.

I have tried to repeat this experience with no success.

I don't know what it was that I saw, but I think of it as the warp and woof of God.

CONFESSION OF A SEXIST

I am a sexist.
For some time now, I have felt that women are the superior sex. Some generalities hold up. For the most part, women are gentler and more compassionate. They are more patient and inherently capable of enduring more physical and emotional pain than men. Women are more intuitive than men . . . more rooted in down-to-earth realities. Women live longer, and they're damn sure prettier.

Of course, whether or not you admire the above qualities depends on your values. Increasingly in our hard-driving, competitive society, the female qualities are being devalued. I get a picture of John Wayne saying, "Get out there and compete, little lady. Hop in yore trusty BMW, whup out yore cell phone, hit the dusty expressway and sell, ma'am . . . sell!"

As women strive for economic equality with men, some of them pick up less attractive male characteristics and become coarser and more aggressive. You see it on the roads: Women drivers ramming their cars through traffic, tailgating, blasting their horns and even making obscene gestures at other drivers. I had a personal experience with such a young woman and it inspired me to write the following little verse:

THE FINGER

I was in the left lane
Looking for my turn,
Going a bit too slow,

When a little black car,
With all black glass,
Came up and started to blow.

It was crowding my bumper
Way too close,
So I pulled back to the right,

And it roared on past
In an awful rush,
Not a human face in sight.

In the black glass window
Of the right front door,
A fist appeared, clenched tight.

Its middle finger
Jabbed the air,
And a scarlet nail burned bright.

"Good bye, my dear,"
I said out loud.
"I hope some day you're free,

To stroll a lovely
Country path
In a place where a girl can be

Touched on the cheek
By a summer breeze
And kissed by a man like me."

    It seems to me that our society should encourage men to adopt some of the finer female qualities, instead of encouraging women to adopt the worst male qualities. But then, what do I know? I'm just a man . . . and a sexist at that.

THE "TR" WORDS

I picked up a copy of *Cosmopolitan* in a doctor's waiting room the other day and was amazed at the money, skill and effort that had gone into producing two hundred slick pages of tripe, trivia and trash.

SNOW WHITE AND THE SEVEN DWARFS

The federal government, in its idiot judgment, has seen fit to restrict water flow in shower valves, faucets and toilets. I suppose the goal is to leave the water in the reservoirs longer to give it more time to evaporate.

Recently, at my gym, some of these restricted-flow showerheads were installed. I complained by posting a notice that said that taking a shower now felt like being urinated on by the seven dwarfs. "Presumably," the notice continued, "Snow White is taking care of the ladies' shower!"

The director of the gym had a sense of humor, and we got the old showerheads back.

READING NOVELS FOR INSPIRATION

Just the thought of a good novel makes my spirits rise. The possibility of moving easily into another time and place . . . into another life . . . brings to my mind a feeling of freedom. It's like flying . . . but finding a good novel . . . there's the rub.

What is a good novel, anyway? I suppose everyone has a different answer to this question. My answer lies in another question: Why do people tell stories?

Some time back-along—shortly after the First World War—art became very negative. Artists and writers turned from trying to depict ideals to trying to depict chaos, alienation and degeneracy. Academics and critics, who have a great deal intelligence with which to get confused, supported this trend and it became fashionable. Sadly this trend continues. It has helped to spawn the degenerate pop culture that afflicts our society today.

Much modern fiction is bleak, despairing, alienated or degenerate. I can't read it. Lavish praise for new novels in the *New York Times Book Review* convinces me to try them. After a few pages, I usually feel my life force diminished. I am discouraged. I know that if I continue the book, I will be downright depressed. Often it is not only the content of the book that is depressing, it is the tone of the author's mind and personality. I believe that reading a novel is as much about getting to know the author as it is about getting to know the characters. Most authors of modern fiction are people I don't want to know. It is better not to read discouraging stories by discouraging writers.

A friend of mine points out that in the days of prehistory people must have sat around the campfire telling stories.

He believes they did this to encourage each other. "Surely they didn't sit around the fire and try to discourage each other!" he says. I agree with him.

People also told stories in order to bond. Stories connect us with each other and with loved ones in the past. They help give continuity to life.

The best novels tell stories that show people connecting. They show us people encouraging each other in adversity and sharing the joys and pains of life. There may be characters that are evil, or a complex mix of good and evil, but I want no moral ambivalence in the character of the author. The best novels inspire, and this inspiration can only come from the mind of an author who is strong and clear in the vision that life, while not easy, is still fundamentally good.

There is another mysterious power often found in good novels . . . their ability to engage the reader. This is perceived as a welcoming. Being drawn into a novel by an engaging writer is like coming to a home on a cold night and being invited into a warmly lit room where a fire is burning and an old friend is waiting by the hearth. You can feel it in a single page or in one paragraph . . . even in a line. It is often felt most strongly when the writer is using the first person . . . "Call me Ishmael."

If I don't feel something engaging, positive or uplifting in the first few pages of a novel—some goodness of character and vision in the author—then I know the book is not for me.

Then there's the whole question of craftsmanship and clarity. How well does a writer write? How clearly does he or she write? Clarity is difficult to achieve, but it is fundamental to good writing. If a reader has to struggle to understand what has been written, the writer has not done his job. Once again I believe that clarity in writing results from the quality of the writer's mind and vision. Muddled writing comes from a muddled mind.

Lately there has come a stupid fad of narrating novels in the present tense. Even newscasters have started to narrate the news in the present tense in an attempt to make the news seem more immediate. Telling a story in the present tense is fundamentally dishonest. The instant something happens, it is in the past, and the only honest way to tell of a past happening is with the past tense. If I open a novel and read something like "I am looking out of my office window and see a young woman getting out of her car. . ." I drop the book like a hot rock.

My own experience is that reading for inspiration means that I have to go to the past. With a few exceptions, I have not been able to find inspiring contemporary fiction. Many of the best books from the past are out of print, so anyone who wants to find inspiring novels from the past will have to poke around old bookstores and libraries. This kind of search is more likely to be fruitful if one has a list of favorite authors and titles.

Here is a list of some of my personal favorites. Since I don't aspire to be a critic, I have included only brief comments:

MARK TWAIN (American)
The Adventures of Huckleberry Finn
It has to be said that the section at the end of this book—where Tom and Huck contrive elaborate schemes to rescue Jim—is a bit tedious.
Tom Sawyer

JOHN GALSWORTHY (English)
The Forsyth Saga (composed of three trilogies)
Galsworthy was a superb craftsman. Every chapter can stand alone.

A BOX OF TRINKETS

KENNETH GRAHAME (English)
  The Wind in the Willows
This "children's" novel is really for all ages. It is unique, funny, heart-warming and inspiring.

J. B. PRIESTLEY (English)
  The Good Companions • *Lost Empires*
These two books are satisfying to read. Priestley wrote well and was very human. He was also a fine essayist.

A. J. CRONIN (English)
  A Song of Sixpence • *The Green Years*
  The Citadel • *A Pocketful of Rye*
Cronin was a medical doctor. He was afflicted with a very rigid Catholic morality but what a writer!

WILLA CATHER (American)
  O Pioneers! • *My Antonia*
  The Song of the Lark • *Death Comes For the Archbishop*
Willa Cather is the most inspiring writer I have read.

MILDRED WALKER (American)
  Winter Wheat

LOUIS BROMFIELD (American)
  Early Autumn • *The Green Bay Tree*
  Possession • *The Rains Came* • *Night in Bombay*
Though much of his writing is about disillusion, Bromfield always has a strong impulse toward renewal and discovering new meaning in life. He is a wonderful, satisfying writer.

JOHN STEINBECK (American)
Cannery Row • Sweet Thursday
I cite two of his lesser works because they are the most uplifting. They are funny and fun.

KENNETH ROBERTS (American)
Arundel • Rabble in Arms
These books are very engaging. They have a wonderful feeling for early New England and create a first-hand experience of the American Revolution. Men seem to like them better than women.

RAY BRADBURY
Dandelion Wine
Ray Bradbury's prose is magical and poetic but still clear! Remarkable!

HARPER LEE (American)
To Kill a Mockingbird
This is the best novel of the South that I know.

HOWARD SPRING (English)
There is No Armour • The Houses In Between
A Sunset Touch • These Lovers Fled Away
Time And the Hour • All the Day Long
I Met a Lady • Winds of the Day
Howard Spring—for years a reporter for the *Manchester Guardian*—wrote with great clarity. His good character and values shine through these pastoral novels. No one described the beauty of unspoiled England better than he did.

HOWARD SPRING, NOVELIST

    Spring, indeed!
    A source of pure, clear prose
    Flowing from the Cornish countryside,
    Reflecting back a pastoral way of life
    Threatened by machines and war,
    Reflecting English hearts and minds
    At their very best.
    Refreshment for the thirsty soul

SEXCOUPLETS

LOUSY LOVER

Ineffectual
In matters sexual.

TRADE-OFF

Her jeans are molded to her rear.
My poor libido's edgy.
Sexy? Yes. Comfort? No.
My kids call it "a wedgy"!

THE GIRL IN THE SUPERMARKET

She's a stunning, sexy beauty
Who knows she has a duty
To attract all males beyond the age of three.

Predictably, I stare
See a haughty toss of hair
Which clearly says, "How dare you look at me!"

THERE'S NO JUSTICE

The perfect man has character.
He's honest, kind and true.
He helps around the kitchen
Like an equal ought to do.

Yet Nicholson could tell you
The way most women feel . . .
It is the rogues
Who have the sex appeal!

TROUBLE

The biggest cause of trouble
That I have ever known
Is something that I make myself
My own testosterone!

HETEROSEXUAL

There's no way that I could possibly be
Attracted to someone constructed like me!

THE EMPEROR'S BLUE CLOTHES

A blue short story

My name's Peter Phillips. I go by Pete, which is more masculine than Peter—a name that should be restricted to the English upper classes. I am an artist and also run the Grayson Gallery, one of the more prestigious art galleries in San Francisco. Jennifer Grayson, one of the make-or-break big shots in the art world, decides what is to be hung in the gallery and she trusts me to hang it. She has never chosen to show any of my work. For the most part, I do semi-abstract Western landscapes. I am a graduate of the Yale Art School and have worked hard to learn how to handle light, color and form. My landscapes are powerful and sell well enough for me to make a living, but they sell in the range of five hundred to a thousand dollars while works that are hung in the Grayson are on the cutting edge of what is considered great art by the wealthy few who decide such things and often sell in the million-dollar range. There was one "painting," a plain white canvas called "White on White" that sold for one and a half million.

I knew that I wasn't going to be able to handle such idiocy much longer, but it was the rolling blue girl that finally pushed me over the edge.

Anne Compton had purchased a work done by an "artist" who called himself Dake. This young man had become the darling of the art world. He was slender and dark with Mediterranean looks—black eyes with long lashes—and he always wore a one-piece black jumpsuit. No one knew where he had come from, but he had been adopted as the leader of the neo-modern movement. He was seen at all the right parties where he maintained an aloof and brooding silence in the grip, no doubt, of his next great idea. Anne Compton had purchased his last work for three and a half million dollars. The work was called "Blue Joy." Dake had coated a young woman with blue paint and she had rolled across a twelve-by-six-foot canvas. Anne Compton and my boss, Jennifer Grayson, had decided to introduce this Dake to the critics with a one-man show and hang only one work . . . "Blue Joy." I now had this canvas in the gallery workroom waiting for the show that was going to be in ten days. Even though there was no artistic value to "Blue Joy," the approval of the critics was a foregone conclusion. In our culture, three and a half million dollars is enough to validate almost anything.

"It's the emperor's new clothes," I told my fiancée, Laura Burns. "Nobody will dare to say that Anne Compton has paid three and a half million for a work that is absolutely worthless. I can't stand it any longer, sweetheart. This is the last show I hang in the Grayson Gallery." Laura was cooking lasagna in my little kitchen in the loft I had converted into a studio and apartment. She put her glass of wine down on the counter and looked at me skeptically. Laura was a potter whose work reflected her own rock-like integrity. She hated my involvement with the phony part of the art world.

"You're really going to quit, Pete?" she asked me. "I'm not sure I believe you. If you intend to quit, why not quit before you hang that piece of nonsense?"

"I want to go out with a bang," I told her, "but I need your help." She raised her eyebrows.

"Uh oh," she said. "Sounds like trouble."

"Yep," I agreed. "Take off your clothes."

I went to the bathroom and returned with some large tubes of blue acrylic paint that had been soaking in a sink full of hot water. I went to the end of my studio and unrolled a twelve-by-six-foot piece of canvas on the floor. Laura stepped out of her panties and stood looking down at it.

"Oh," she said, grinning, "I see."

"Exactly," I agreed. "This is going to be a bit messy," I said, squirting out a handful of warm, blue paint. I worked fast.

"Now I lie down, I presume," Laura said.

"Right," I said, "and roll slowly to the other end. Make it interesting. Change your arm and leg positions as you roll." She did as I asked.

"Magnificent!" I said. "Truly great art. I didn't know you had it on you. Quick, darling, jump in the shower. This stuff dries fast. Bring the rest of the paint out of the sink when you come out." She came back wrapped in a towel. I had my clothes off and had unrolled another canvas.

"You too?" she asked, beginning to laugh.

"Equality of the sexes, my dear," I told her. "Get to work."

Laura began to coat me with the warm paint. As she smoothed it on, there was a predictable reaction.

"I think I am going to make a somewhat phallic impression on the canvas," I told her. I was right. I rolled out three repetitions.

"Oh dear," she said, looking down at me as we both got in the shower. "I think we're going to have to do something about that. We don't want it to become permanent."

"Well . . . OK," I said with feigned indifference. "If you insist."

Of course, when the show opened, the three canvases were a huge sensation. I hung Dake's canvas, "Blue Joy," between Laura's canvas and mine. Laura's canvas was titled, "Nude Indigo" and under my "self portrait" I had written the somewhat folksy inscription:

"Over the hill and across the creek
Came a blue-balled bastard named Piss Pot Pete!"

I DREAM THAT I AM BIX'S DAD

For Bix Beiderbecke, jazz cornetist (1903–1931)

Bix drank himself to death.
When he was still a young man,
Sadness took him.
His father wouldn't help . . .
Couldn't love.

Once when Bix went home
He found the records he had sent his dad.
Unopened.
Now, I listen . . .
Marveling at the silliness—
Moaning vocal . . .
Syrupy sax . . .
Ricky-ticky banjo . . .
High-hat cymbal like a sneezing Chihuahua—
Then . . .
Up jumps Bix!
His golden notes pushing towards ecstasy
(As Condon said:)
"Like a girl saying 'yes.'"
The silliness is gone.
Magically, the band transforms.

It's then I dream that I am Bix's dad.
I hold his shoulders
Smile into his eyes and say,
"I hear you, Son,
I'm proud!"

A SIXTY-YEAR-OLD BOY REMEMBERS TRAINS

(Excerpted in part from *FUN! A Boyhood*)

Never do I board an airplane without wishing I was standing in some gritty station, listening to a steaming, hissing train and stepping on the bright-yellow foot-stool below the bottom step of a Pullman car.

As the relentless march of progress sweeps aside many wonderful things, we have swapped the wonder, adventure and leisure of train travel for the convenience and boredom of planes; a bad bargain, and one that forces this particular sixty-year-old boy to look back to the nineteen forties. I was a little boy then, a boy who was lucky enough to have parents who took him on many overnight trips in Pullman cars. As I remember, I can smell the steam, feel the excitement and hear the wonderful double click-clack as the train rolls out into the open countryside.

We would arrive at the station and, as a redcap loaded our bags onto a wooden hand truck with iron wheels, I, bursting with excitement, would run ahead into the station.

The Terminal Station in Birmingham, Alabama was an exotic and marvelous place. Long pewlike wooden benches were dwarfed by the huge, domed space of the waiting area. The light was always silvery, being filtered through large smoke-grayed windows and echoing through the marble-columned space would be the dry, tinny, singsong announcements:

"Departing from Track 10, The Silver Comet. All aboard for . . ." and the announcer would reel off a list of mysterious towns and cities all strung together so you couldn't understand them.

Train names sparkled with adventure: the Silver Comet, the Silver Star, the Silver Meteor, the Birmingham Special, the City of Miami, the Southerner. . . .

There was a newsstand in an alcove to the right of the gates. The alcove was dim and dingy with overhead lights hanging down in the gloom and there, in front of the counter stacked in wooden racks, glowing with color and smelling of fresh printer's ink, was the ultimate selection of comic books. All the best ones were there from Donald Duck through Batman and Plastic Man. I would have a dollar and a quarter for comics! Six hundred and twenty-four pages of glorious color, fantasy and adventure! What a satisfying bulk to hold.

Finally, Mother and Dad, my sister Caroline and I would all go through the gate. A short walk to the right would lead us to stairs going underground into a dimly lit tunnel. Tiny chips of mica sparkled in the steps and in the asphalt floor of the tunnel. We would climb the steps to the track and, as we emerged into the daylight, there would be the train hissing and steaming in all its power and grimy, olive-green majesty.

Sometimes we would emerge onto the platform as the engine was pulling in. Watching it stop with a clanking, hissing jerk, I would be awestruck. Its massive pistons, wheels and cowcatcher, clanging bell and intricacy of valves pipes and fittings might have been designed especially to fascinate a small boy. The masters of these behemoths, the engineers, in their corded denim caps and red bandannas, could usually be counted on to return a grin and a wave.

Often the Pullman cars would be towards the end of the train. There was always a yellow box with stubby legs used to help passengers reach the bottom step of the car. When I climbed aboard, my anticipation would melt into pure satisfaction, as I became part of the train.

A Pullman car smelled unlike any place else on earth. A combination of coal smoke, tobacco smoke and disinfectant from the men's room, the cool metal of the car, the upholstery, the heating or air-conditioning—all these things and more—combined to envelop you.

Most Pullman cars in those days were about two-thirds seats, which converted to berths, and one-third compartments and bedrooms. My sister, Caroline, and I would each have a berth, but Mother and Dad always had a compartment. Between reading comics and playing cards—"hearts"—with Caroline and Mother and Dad on a table set up in their compartment, I would gaze out the window as the world unrolled before my eyes: a different world from the one seen from an automobile.

You would find yourself looking into the backyard of a rural shack at a woman using a stick to stir laundry in a black, iron pot or, when the train slowed as it pulled into a city, you might find yourself peering into the tiny kitchen of some poor flat and watching a family eat dinner. You would roll behind factories, amid the junk, through wild, beautiful swamps and across farm fields and rivers. Tunnels would scarily plunge you without warning into noisy blackness. Another thrill was a long, gentle curve when you could look ahead and see the engine trailing great puffs of smoke. If you had a lower berth, you might wake in the night as the train pulled into some deserted station. Pinching together the two metal tabs to raise the shade a few inches, you could peer through the steam and yellow lights to watch some solitary trainman swinging his lantern as he checked the train. As the train rolled on through the night, you might peer out and see a farmhouse huddled in the moonlight or the empty main street of a little country town. Such lonely scenes would make you feel extra snug in your berth as you drifted off to the rhythmic swaying and double click-clack of the wheels.

Everything about a train was fascinating. The ladder you needed for an upper berth, the little green net hammock for clothing, the black ventilator nozzle that could be twisted to direct the air, the small round reading light which could be switched to be a mysterious, glowing, blue night-light, the way the porter rolled the extra blanket; all these things seemed to be there for my particular enjoyment.

For those passengers who had a berth, there was a ladies' room and a men's room. The ladies, requiring more privacy, had a door into their room. The men had a curtain. Short of a football locker room, there were few places more uncompromisingly masculine than the men's room on a Pullman car. Pushing the curtain aside, you would see to the left a black leather seat that ran the length of the room. Facing you between the windows were two shiny metal sinks for washing and shaving and to the right was another little sink for drinking water and the door to the toilet. To flush the toilet you stepped on a little pedal, and the bottom of the toilet flipped down to reveal the rail bed whisking by. A little sign near the toilet admonished, "Passengers will please refrain from flushing toilet while the train is standing in the station." There was always a shiny, brass spittoon, and there were usually men in their undershirts shaving and smoking cigars. All in all, it was a place a young boy felt barely qualified to enter!

Then there would be excursions to the dining car or the club car. On your way to the dining car you would be turned around by a little blue sign at the end of the Pullman car. It said, "Dining car in opposite direction." (Reader, do you remember what was on the back side of the little, blue sign? If not, I will tell you later.)

Moving between cars was exciting. Pushing open the heavy doors at the end of the car, you would be hit by a wave of noise that made talking impossible. Getting to the next car meant crossing several shifting, sliding steel plates with nothing much to hold on to.

Dining cars were all different and yet all the same. There was always a "steward" in a blue uniform who was in charge of seating people. While waiting, you might get a peek into the stainless steel kitchen, a marvel of compactness, and see the white uniformed cooks at work. Sometimes you were seated with strangers. This was horrifying at first but usually proved to be interesting. The food always had a kind of greasy, smoky taste but was always good and sometimes excellent. Tables were set with snowy white tablecloths and napkins and heavy silver, china and glassware. Rough roadbeds and sudden stops and starts meant there were lots of spills that meant frequent changes of the tablecloths. The waiters could accomplish this with amazing dexterity.

I remember one waiter whose job it was to provide room service by taking trays of food and drink to the Pullman cars. He carried the laden trays balanced on his head on a cloth ring. This left his hands free to open the heavy doors between the cars. As this waiter passed through the train, he kept his head perfectly still compensating for the lurching of the train by swinging his hips with the combined grace of a ballet dancer and a broken-field-runner. It was a wonderful performance to watch.

On trains, and everywhere else in those days, black people did the menial work. Porters and waiters not only had hard work and long hours but also had to be away from home for days at a time. At the time, I took all of this for granted, but now I look back with great admiration for the black people who did such hard jobs with skill and reliability and somehow managed to retain their warmth and humanity.

The club car was the last car on the train, and on the end of the club car was a little "balcony" called the platform. Usually the door to the platform was left unlocked, and you could stand out there and smell the lush greenness of the passing countryside and watch the steel rails spin out under you into the distance. They kept a box of flares out there that looked intriguingly like sticks of dynamite. Each flare had a sharp steel spike on one end. They were lit and stuck in a crosstie to signal other trains.

I think I first became aware of the relativity of motion on trains. Sometimes you would be in a station staring out the window at another train stopped alongside. The train you were watching or your own train would start to move very smoothly, but there was no way to tell which train was moving. Very disorienting! Or, you might pass another train going at a high speed in the opposite direction. The combined speeds of the two trains would be over a hundred miles an hour and, since the two trains were only a few feet apart, the other train would blast past in a breathtaking, whooshing blur.

Did other boys marvel at the way the sag in the telephone lines caused them to swoop up and down as the train passed? Did they hold up one hand and—closing one eye—let it scythe down passing telephone poles? I expect they did. Sometimes I would pick out a leaf on a tree and, examining it carefully as we passed, I would think, "That leaf was just twenty feet away. I know it was there but I could not touch it. Now it is gone and I will never see it again." These kinds of thoughts may have presaged a slight philosophical bent. Certainly they indicated a budding awareness of the impermanent, transitory nature of life. And if life were not transitory, dear reader, we would still have our wonderful trains carrying small boys on their own odysseys across this great land of ours.

Ah yes, I promised to tell you what was on the back of the little blue sign. The other side said, "Have you forgotten any personal property?" . . . and yes, I did forget something. I left my heart on The Birmingham Special!

MY TURTLE'S IN THE TOILET

(My most popular children's poem)

My turtle's in the toilet,
And every time I flush,
He swims against the current.
He gets in quite a rush.

A turtle in the toilet
Is such a big surprise . . .
I put him there from time to time
To get his exercise!

ROSE

We had taken my mother-in-law, Rose Marshall, to Golden City, our favorite Chinese restaurant. Being from a Cornish village, she was quite impressed with the décor. When our food came, she was still looking around. I spotted some of the hot little dried red peppers on her plate.

"Rose, don't eat those," I said, pointing at the peppers.

"Oh, this is a lovely café," she replied in her Cornish accent, gazing around the room.

"Rose! Listen!" I said. "Don't eat the red peppers!"

"Lovely décor!" She replied, looking at the ceiling.

I saw that I wasn't getting through so I scooped up one of the peppers in a spoon and held it under her nose.

"Rose! See this?" I said. "Don't eat these!" She still didn't look.

"Yes, yes," she said vaguely.

"She isn't listening," my wife said.

"I are!" said Rose.

Yep . . . on the first bite . . . Rose ate a pepper.

She grabbed the ice out of her water glass and packed it into her mouth. Soon she had exhausted all the ice on the table. A waiter was passing.

"More ice! More ice!" She told him desperately.

The young Chinese waiter rushed off and returned very quickly with a steaming platter of rice.

It could only happen to Rose.

TO AN ENGLISH SOLDIER

My father-in-law, Don Fisher, died yesterday. I was very fond of him. We shared some wonderful times together.

He was strong but kind and patient, and he had a sense of fun that I really enjoyed. More than this, I admired Don. He was such a "tough old bird." He was staunch.

When I first met Don, he was in his early sixties. He and my mother-in-law, Rose, came to visit my wife, Jill, and me in Vero Beach, Florida. I was amazed when he tossed Rose (one hundred sixty pounds) over his shoulder and galloped around our garden while the sprinkler system was running.

Don wasn't just physically tough. He survived some very hard emotional knocks.

His mother died when he was seven, and when he had his own family, his wife died suddenly . . . leaving him to bring up eight children. He accomplished this in spite of having a very limited income.

When Don was a young man, along came World War II. Even though youngsters don't know it today, that war had to be won. Don was one of the young men who "bellied up to the bar" and did what had to be done. He made eighty-nine parachute jumps, three of which were into combat in North Africa, Italy and Holland where he was captured and spent a year in a German prison camp.

It's not enough to say we owe a lot to the men who fought that war. We owe them everything. I'm glad I had a chance to thank Don for what he did for us.

Don got a great deal of pleasure out of life. He loved sport and he loved gadding about with Rose. (There may be a corner of Cornwall that they didn't get into, but I wouldn't bet on it.)

Once he spent an hour trying to explain cricket to me. When he finished—to my wife's great amusement—I understood absolutely nothing!

Don and Rose made friends wherever they went. There are a number of people in Alabama who will miss him a lot. I'm one of them.

MY OTHER HALF

I dreamed, one night, a game of hide-and-seek.
I, a man of almost fifty years,
Played with her, a girl of five—
Dainty, dark, gamine . . . a gentle sprite.
In seeking me, she trod with care
The timbers of a part-constructed house.
I did not need to hide,
For she was blind.
I sat and waited quietly in her path.
Concerned that I would give her fright,
I softly spoke,
"I'm here . . . ahead," I said,
And I was found.
We hugged, and I was sure I would adopt this child,
And she would have to seek no more.

THE SKEPTICAL BELIEVER
(All Bible quotes are from the New International Version Bible)

Some time ago I came to the conclusion that Christ taught a very demanding way of life. Reading Matthew, I see that what Christ taught was, in fact, so demanding that nobody could or would live it. Lately I have concluded that going to church is the way people try to have their cake and eat it, that is, try to stay right with God without having to live the demands of Christ. For example, in Matthew, 6:19-21, Christ admonishes not to store up treasures on earth, but heck, we all store up treasures on earth. Look at the luxury cars outside the church and the Rolex watches and diamond rings within. You have to wonder what a poor Jewish carpenter would make of it.

Then there is the passage about not worrying about bodily needs in Matthew 6:25-34. While I agree that it is useless to worry, some of the examples in this passage don't make sense to me.

The passage says the birds don't sow or reap. That's true, but birds work their little tail feathers off feeding themselves and their young. If they don't worry, it is probably because they're too busy!

Then there's the idea that the lilies "do not labor or spin." Well, yes . . . but you shouldn't compare them to us. We don't have the advantage of photosynthesis!

There are some astounding contradictions between Christ's teachings and Christian religious services.

In Matthew 6:1-6, we are admonished not to give or pray publicly. If you consider the taking up the collection as public giving (which it surely is) and hymns as musical prayer (which most of them are), then—taking into account all the long-winded prayers from the pulpit—two-thirds of your average church service is directly contrary to Christ's admonitions. Well, there's still the sermon. Christ did seem to approve of sermons.

I never have understood the long-winded prayers, anyway. Prayers that are full of praising, thanking and beseeching seem to me to be an attempt to manipulate God . . . as if He can't be trusted to do the right thing. God is treated as if He is some oriental potentate who might chop off your head if you don't approach him properly. There is an admonition attributed to Jesus that agrees with this:

"And when you pray, do not keep on babbling like pagans, for they think that they will be heard for their many words. Do not be like them, for your Father knows what things you need before you ask him." Matthew 6:7-8

I wonder if all these groveling, long-winded prayers that you hear on the radio and on television come from an inner knowledge that those who are doing the praying are ignoring many of Christ's teachings.

Then there's the real toughie: "Do not judge . . ." Matthew 7:1. We all have a hard time with this, yet many Christians seem absolutely obsessed with how morally wrong other folks are. I've heard Christians say that homosexuals who have A.I.D.S. deserve it. On the other hand, I know some wonderfully compassionate and nonjudgmental Christians. Personally, I much prefer these Christians to the Christians who are obsessed with the specks in other folks' eyes.

Speaking of "eyes," in Matthew 5:29-30, after being taught that looking at a woman lustfully is tantamount to adultery we are told that "if your right eye causes you to sin, gouge it out and throw it away," and, "if your right hand causes you to sin, cut it off and throw it away." No point, really, in keeping it!

Well, durn! Not being a keyhole peeper, I, for one, look lustfully with both eyes, and I don't have the slightest intention of gouging them out nor of cutting off either hand nor do I blame Christians for passing lightly over these particular admonitions!

The Way is impossibly hard. Anyone who tries to follow it is going to wind up a hypocrite somewhere along the line—double trouble, because there are a number of admonitions against hypocrisy.

If you're a fundamentalist, you're really up a creek. Fundamentalists are supposed to take everything literally but they accumulate riches, pray publicly, give publicly and how many one-eyed or one-handed fundamentalists do you know? Can it be that they don't read Matthew?

In the Bible, there are some wonderful guidelines for living. Forgiveness, for example, may be the most powerful spiritual tool that we have. And you certainly need help from the Holy Spirit to achieve it. I try to use this one. On the other hand, "Be perfect . . ." Matthew 5:48 is—like self-mutilation—another one that I pass over. It's a terrible strain trying to be perfect. "Muddle through" is more my way, trusting that others—including God—will forgive my mistakes.

Is skepticism nonspiritual? A touch of skepticism might be helpful to those who choose to follow televangelists.

> (Two great T.V. preachers named Jim
> Claimed a special connection with Him.
> But when push came to shove
> The light from above
> Turned out to be frightfully dim!)

I think God gave me the power to discriminate, and so I use it to pick the workable life principles out of the Bible and I skip the rest. Since my brain is less than perfect, I make mistakes but, as long as I own up to them, I'm at least saved from hypocrisy.

When I was writing this little piece, I asked a close friend of mine who is a committed Christian for criticism on what I had written. He told me that the rather extreme admonitions in Matthew are Christ speaking metaphorically. For example, if someone says: "I'd like to give him a piece of my mind," it is not meant literally. "Piece of my mind" is a metaphor equal to "tongue lashing" or "chewing out" all of which mean reprimand. I am willing to grant that the admonitions about cutting off hands and plucking out eyes should be read as metaphors. Certain statements, however, have a very direct quality.

"If you don't put your hands up, I'll shoot!" for example, has this direct quality and needs to be taken literally. Admonitions like: *Don't pray publicly* and *Don't give alms publicly* have this direct quality. They do not feel like metaphors. If you say these admonitions are metaphors, then you can say the same about any teaching in the bible. If one direct statement is a metaphor, why couldn't any teaching be considered a metaphor? Worse than this, once you say a direct statement is a metaphor, you have to ask what the metaphor means and this opens the door to interpretation—I think it means this; you think it means that; and he thinks it means something else. As soon as this happens, you need lots of denominations to accommodate all the different opinions.

My Christian friend also told me that the parts about giving secretly and praying privately were intended for the posturing Pharisees, but if the Pharisees gave in to the temptation to feel holier-than-thou and superior, why couldn't the rest of us fall into the same error? I remember feeling pretty puffed up and holy back during my churchgoing days. If we think we're so much better than the Pharisees, haven't we already become like them?

These last thoughts are couched as questions, because I don't have all the answers. As a "skeptical believer," I don't have to have all the answers. Thank goodness I don't have to have all the answers. I couldn't come up with them.

In spite of my doubts and questions about the Bible, much of it rings true. Behind all the inconsistencies, a picture of an extraordinary, charismatic man emerges. A man whose love accepted whores, tax collectors, thieves and all the other sinners who, like you and me, were so far short of perfection. Such a man is certainly worthy of great love and loyalty.

I can sum all of this up with a two-line verse I call:

THE SKEPTICAL BELIEVER

I believe, but I ain't no pigeon.
God made man, but man made religion.

THE WRONG DUCK

My first wife's father, Johnny Oberg, was a character. A short, amazingly wiry Swede, Johnny had been at sea for most of his life. When he came to the States, he wound up as a steward on yachts. A self-taught horticulturist, superb cook and raconteur without equal, he spent most of his time on the yachts. His wife and three children lived in a little house on Northwest Fourteenth Street in Miami. During World War II, John worked as a cook in the Biltmore Air Force Hospital and was able to live at home for a change.

The family had a pet duck that went missing. The children were grief stricken, and John and his wife searched the neighborhood in vain. After three days, the duck still had not turned up. Finally, one misty, early morning when he was driving to work, he saw the duck in someone's yard. He quickly parked and eased himself out of the car, planning a strategic approach so that he could reach the duck without alarming it. Creeping from one group of bushes to the next, Johnny Oberg finally reached the short hedge that the duck was behind. In the dim light he could just make it out through the foliage. He eased up as close as he dared, leaped over the hedge and grabbed the duck around its neck. The duck was made of concrete . . . a yard ornament.

When Johnny told me this story, he would narrow his eyes and look over his shoulder showing me how quickly he had looked around to see who had watched him pounce on the concrete duck.

"Oh, Al," he would say in his thick Swedish accent, "thank God no vun vas vatching!"

I know the feeling. When we feel really stupid, we surely don't want anyone watching.

A BOX OF TRINKETS

Recently I was checking out at the supermarket and there was a stunningly beautiful woman in the next line over. She preceded me out of the market and was parked near my car, so I had a chance to follow her through the parking lot. The view from behind was by far the most advantageous!

I got to my car, opened the trunk and reached into my shopping cart. No groceries. I'm sure the feeling was very much like pouncing on a concrete duck.

THE CHAIN OF LIFE

(A calypso song recorded by my Bahamian friend, Barry Ward—who also wrote the music)

The bee comes down to the bush to drink up the nectar.
The bird comes down to the bush to eat up the bee.
The cat she eat up the bird like you would expect her.
That's called the chain of life. It's the way things be.

The crab eat up all the things way down on the bottom.
The fish eat up all the crab that he gonna see.
The man eat up all the fish when the man has got 'em.
That's called the chain of life. It's the way things be.

But the man catch up too many fish.
He's breaking the sacred chain.
When all the fish are gone from the sea,
He gonna sure complain.

The mouse eat up all the seed and the fat grasshopper.
The snake he eat up the mouse in the banyan tree.
The hawk she grab up the snake. Don't you try to stop her.
That's called the chain of life. It's the way things be.

THOUGHTS ON WRITING 'MY BROTHER'S STORY'

In 1998 I began working on *My Brother's Story*, a book that I hoped would be a novel for adults. (I don't dare use the term "adult novel," because the term "adult" now means pornographic.)

Since I am primarily a children's writer, I was not completely sure I could pull this off. When *My Brother's Story* was finished in 1999, it became clear that I had failed. It seems I had written a "young adult" novel. After the book was published, however, I was comforted to discover that the "young adult" label was really a marketing designation and that my book transcends age and appeals to the young at heart of all ages.

My Brother's Story is the story of identical twin boys who are separated when they are two-and-a-half years old. It is about their struggle to get back together.

My own boyhood was idyllic, but underneath the fun, there was a dark aspect to my childhood. Possibly the theme of reuniting twins—one privileged and one deprived—may reflect my own attempt to integrate the idyllic and the dark parts of my own past. This aside, however, I have always been fascinated by the idea of having an identical twin.

We all are alone in the world. Our aloneness is softened by the empathy and understanding of those who love us, but there is no one who completely knows our hearts and souls.

Identical twins are different. They share a closeness that transcends the aloneness the rest of us experience. Also, in exploring the nature versus nurture question, it is interesting to examine the lives of twins who have been separated and who have grown up under very different conditions.

In my book, the twins theme runs parallel to the theme of love between the races in the South. This too reflects my past in which I was loved and supported by the black people who helped to bring me up.

When I lived in the Northeast, I ran across intellectuals who didn't believe that love between the races existed in the South during the time of segregation. They told me I had mistaken Uncle Tomism for love. They were wrong. Deep affection and respect was common between good black people and good white people in the South—probably more than anywhere else in the country—in spite of the vile social system of segregation. This fact is a testimony that love can transcend the most difficult barriers.

In *My Brother's Story*, the relationship between Linc and Johnny is based on the goodness of both characters. As they live and work together, they come to know each other. As they help and comfort each other, inevitably they come to love each other.

The idea of goodness leads to an important issue. In modern times moral ambivalence has become fashionable in fiction—even in children's fiction. Characters are considered "two-dimensional" if they are clearly good or clearly bad. Children love good good guys and bad bad guys, however. I will go so far as to say children need moral clarity in their stories. They need ideals. The Lone Ranger was ridiculously good. In fact, he was perfect. I loved him when I was a boy. Even today, the shining nobility of the Lone Ranger captivates my own little boy. Linc is not perfect, but he is an essentially good man. He is a man you can count on to do the right thing, and I make this quite clear in *My Brother's Story*. I believe that stories that have moral clarity help protect and reinforce the innocence of children. The experience of going into schools on author visits and reading to kids has given me a firsthand chance to observe how thousands of children react to my characters and has convinced me that I am giving them what they need.

Another goal I had when I wrote *My Brother's Story* was to show the richness of life as it existed in the South before World War II. I wanted to show how extended families were woven together by storytelling. To do this I drew on stories that were told around my grandparents' dinner table or at family suppers on their pavilion.

I also wanted to show how children made their own fun in those days. There was no adult-structured play in those days. The pursuit of fun—a child's proper occupation—was spontaneous, creative and—in the case of boys—often involved the tantalizing risk of getting into trouble.

My Brother's Story tells of some wonderful things that existed in the 1930s that we no longer have . . . a profusion of fireflies, for example. It is by no means nostalgia when I say that it was magical to watch hundreds and hundreds of fireflies sparking in the soft summer twilight. I don't know what has happened to this phenomenon in the South. It's possible that fireflies fell victim to pesticides.

My book also shows in some detail the wonderful joys of train travel. When I was growing up, our country had a rail system that was the envy of the world. Trains, most of which had Pullman cars with sleeping accommodations, served thousands of towns and cities efficiently. Our passenger rail system is no more but, if I have done my job well, those who read *My Brother's Story* can still enjoy the thrill and adventure of a train trip.

The way of life that existed in the Thirties and Forties was better in some ways than the way we live today. With the exception of modern medicine, modern automobiles and computers, I would swap the way of life in 2001 for the 1940s' way, if such a thing were possible. Lacking the ability to move back in time, however, I can at least try in my writing to preserve the memories of what life was like when I was a boy. *My Brother's Story* should help give young readers a sense of continuity with the past.

Who knows . . . someday, when technology becomes more transparent, there may be a return to a more pastoral way of life. *My Brother's Story* may help point the way to a slower, richer way of living . . . a way in which we have the time to be more connected with our natural world and with each other. Meanwhile, my hopes are much less grandiose than this. I simply hope to continue to hear that the young at heart of all ages consider *My Brother's Story* a good yarn.

POTATO SOUP SURPRISE

(This poem illustrates the intimate connection
between boyhood fun and getting into trouble!)

My sister was a pretty girl who always tried to please.
While I was just a scruffy boy with dirty, skint-up knees.
My sister, being starched and clean, was purely made to tease.
So this is how the whole thing came to be.

I was sitting on the porch and talking to my frog.
"Zeb," I says—he looked at me adoring, like a dog.
"It's hot. You should be in a pond, a-diving off a log,"
And that was when the idea came to me.

"Supper!" Momma hollered, and it being mighty hot,
She'd chilled up some potato soup in Grandma's old clay pot.
"My, my," I thought, "to cool a frog, that soup should hit the spot!
Let's have some fun!" I says to Zebbidee.

My sister, Grace, sat down to eat a-looking prim and proper
She took a scoop of frog and soup, and Lord it came a slopper!
And then she started in to scream, we couldn't hardly stop her.
And Mamma reached and snatched a hold of me.

Well Zeb, he went back in the pond before a boy could blink.
Potato soup without its frog was all poured down the sink.
And my poor old tail-end-of-things has turned a handsome pink.
But lovely fun don't ever come for free.

MEMORIES OF A CLASSIC YACHT
On Board *Car-Al II*

(Thanks to Norm Wangard, Editor of *Classic Boating* magazine, for permission to reprint this article.)

On December 7, 1941, the day Pearl Harbor was attacked, I was on board my dad's 55-foot Elco yacht, *Car-Al*. I was six years old. I vaguely remember our being stopped by the Coast Guard as we approached Pensacola, Florida. Several months after this the Navy took Dad's boat to use on coastal patrols. I have no other memories of the first *Car-Al*.

Shortly after the war was over, Dad acquired his second yacht and afflicted me with a lifelong love of boating.

Car-Al II, like Dad's original boat, was named after my sister Caroline and me. She was a sixty-five-foot Grebe powerboat, all wood with two two-hundred-horsepower diesels. She carried a captain, a steward and a deckhand, who slept in the small fo'c'sle forward, and she slept six guests aft.

The master stateroom opened onto the cockpit and had twin berths and a head and shower. There were two guest staterooms on the port side with fold-down upper berths. A sliding door could convert the guest staterooms to one room. A guest head and shower were on the starboard side.

When I was a boy, I slept aft as a guest. As a boy, a trip on *Car-Al II* was wall-to-wall fun. As a young man, when the boat was on charter, I slept forward as a deckhand. I found life in both ends of the boat equally satisfying.

A boat trip always started with an overnight train ride to wherever the boat was in Florida, usually Miami. The night in a

Pullman berth was made doubly exciting by my anticipation of the boat trip.

I have always been easily swayed by smells. When I stepped aboard *Car-Al II,* the smell—a mixture of salt air, wood, bath soap, insect spray and diesel fuel—was heady wine indeed. When the engines were started, the lines cast off and the boat slid away from the dock, there would always be a whiff of diesel exhaust . . . a smell that, even today, sends a thrill through me.

Car-Al II had a roomy pilothouse, a comfortable deckhouse with a dining table and dinette forward, a spacious aft deck with rattan furniture and a cushioned seat on the bow . . . a favorite place of mine.

In those days, the inland waterways of Florida were mostly wilderness. I, and whatever buddy was along, would lie up on the bow, peer over at the porpoises playing in the bow wave and watch the ever-changing banks of the waterway. Swamp grass surrounded jungly little hammocks. Herons waded amid the mangroves and clear, brown creeks disappeared mysteriously into the thick tropical growth. We might as well have been on the Amazon.

Seeing another boat was an event. We would run and get *Lloyd's Registry,* a blue volume that listed yachts, who owned them, where they were from, how big they were and the name of the builder. *Lloyds* even had pictures of the owners' personal flags.

There were no modern, concrete marinas in those days. Usually we would tie up to some rickety, wooden dock that had small grunts and snapper teaming around the piling. It would take me about three minutes to grab a rod and some bait and be after them.

Sometimes we would head into the Keys. Mother and Dad were members of a small club on north Key Largo called the Key Largo Angler's Club. It was the only thing on North Key Largo. The club had wooden docks behind a breakwater, a rustic central clubhouse with a large screen porch, a dining room and a long living room with an oil painting of Herbert Hoover—in a boat with his fishing guide—hanging over the fireplace. There were a few cottages scattered around with coconut palms, sea grapes and masses of hibiscus and bougainvillea. The atmosphere of the place was informal and tropical. It was a little paradise tucked away in the middle of nowhere.

One evening, after having dinner in the clubhouse, I wandered out on the front screen porch to waste a few quarters on the slot machine—illegal and hence a rarity. On the third try, I hit the jackpot. Eighteen dollars in silver quarters, a goodly sum in the Forties . . . a satisfying weight of silver. I put the quarters in one of my socks. The manager of the club needed the change and wanted to give me paper money for my quarters. No sir! I was young, but I knew the difference between several slips of paper and seventy-two silver quarters clinking in my pockets and dragging down one side of my pants.

Nights in the Keys were magical. Out of range of city lights, the skies were the blackest velvet. We would lie on our backs on the bow with the fragrant tropical breezes causing the boat to tug gently on her lines and nudge her fenders. Watching the billions of stars in the velvet sky, we'd see one meteor after another streak across the heavens. Often this display in the sky would be mirrored in the water. Clearest turquoise by day, the water would be jet black at night and filled with phosphorescence that would glow when it was agitated. The abundant fish would leave green trails of light that would glow as the fish streaked through the black waters.

Finally we would go below and climb into our bunks. There was no air-conditioning on boats in those days, and we always felt a bit stifled in our bunks—sunburn scratchy on the sheets—but fatigue, salt air and the gentle motion of the boat soon did their work, and we slept like the dead.

From the Anglers Club, we would cruise farther down to

Marathon and tie up at Thompson's Marina where there was a natural swimming pool enclosed by coral rocks. We swam there with large, beautiful parrotfish.

When I was nineteen, my dad decided to charter *Car-Al II* to Henry Sears, vice commodore of the New York Yacht Club. I knew that the crew was shy a deckhand and asked Dad if I could have the job for the summer with the understanding that the charter party would not know that I was the owner's son. This is how I found myself once again aboard *Car-Al II* with two colorful shipmates: tall, blond, balding Captain Larsen, called "Cap," and a short, dark, wiry Swedish steward, John Oberg, called "Johnny."

I met the boat, picked up some khaki uniforms, a cap and a black tie at a uniform place, and moved into the fo'c'sle on *Car-Al II* On the trip from Miami to Glencove, Long Island, I got to know my shipmates. They were both hard-working old salts who took pride in everything being shipshape. Cap, a lugubrious-looking Norwegian with a thick accent, was forever sanding and varnishing. By the time he finished at the bow of the boat, it was time to start back at the stern again. He taught me how to handle lines—which were always flemished—polish brightwork, shammy-mop the deck, check the batteries, splice, steer by the compass and all the other elements of my job. We all worked together. We would help Cap sand and varnish and help Johnny wash and dry the dishes. When we were on our own, the work wasn't demanding. When the charter party was aboard, the days were long and hard.

I had brought along a target pistol and a thousand rounds of ammunition. On the way north, as we cruised at eight knots through the bays and marshes of the inland waterways, I would sit on the bow and pop away at waterbirds skimming the surface a hundred yards ahead of the boat. Of course, I never hit one. The goal was to make one change course.

Cap was delightful. He tended to be windy and would break

wind loudly as he worked. When he did this, he'd laugh and say, "Slack away aft!" He usually whistled while he worked and sometimes played the harmonica.

Johnny, who was to become my father-in-law, was an artist in the galley and a gifted storyteller. Like most young men in those days, I smoked. Johnny taught me to roll my own cigarettes out of Prince Albert pipe tobacco. I would sit for hours with him at the galley table, rolling smokes and listening to sea yarns. I remember two that fascinated me.

In the early part of the war, Johnny had shipped out on an ammunition barge that was towed across the Atlantic. For safety reasons, the towline was so long that the ocean-going tug was almost out of sight.

Another time he signed up to cook on a lightship that was moored off the Massachusetts coast. There was a sonar bell dinging constantly, a teeth-rattling foghorn that went off every minute or so, and each wave brought the ship up against the anchor chain with a terrific jolt. He said there wasn't a sane man in the whole crew.

We ran outside from Norfolk to Long Island, and I learned how difficult it was to steer a good course with a following sea. *Car-Al II* was really meant for the inland waterway. Her bottom was fairly round and she rolled a good bit. We ran all night on that trip. When I took my turn at the wheel, Cap dozed on the long, leather-cushioned seat in the pilothouse. When it was time to wake him, there was no way I could do it without causing him to start up, fearing something was wrong.

We lay in Glencove, New York for almost a week before the charter. One day at the dock, there were three Amazonian young women in bathing suits trying to start a heavy outboard motor on their boat. I watched them wrap and yank the cord for about ten minutes until they were all sweaty and pretty pooped out. At this point, I asked them if I could help. I was a skinny young man. They looked at my physique with scorn and amusement but said I could try. I wrapped the cord. One yank and as the motor started—purring smoothly—I tossed the cord in their boat, smiled and sauntered down the dock whistling. Johnny, who had been watching all this, was hugely tickled by it. He said he never saw anyone get such dirty looks as I got from those young women.

A day or so after this, a boat capsized out in the sound and a man drowned. When the Coast Guard brought the body in, I walked down the dock to see what was going on. I had never seen a corpse before, and a drowning victim is pretty ghastly. When I got back to *Car-Al II*, I must have looked pale. Johnny was on the bow. As they carried the body in a wire basket up the gangway from the dock to the shore, a loose arm was bobbing up and down. Johnny grinned at me and said in his

Swedish accent, "He's vaving at you, Al."

I had to laugh and it broke the tension.

The New York Yacht Club cruise was a racing cruise from port to port around New England. Our charterer, Henry Sears, was racing a thirty-seven-foot yawl. *Car-Al II* provided all the comforts for him and his crew. We would go on ahead to the end point of the race and anchor. After Sears finished the race, he would rendezvous with us, tie his boat alongside *Car-Al II,* and he and his crew would come aboard for drinks, a good meal and a soft bed.

I had a close call with one of these anchorings. I had coiled a couple of hundred feet of line on the forward deck and it was going out fast as the captain backed the boat to get enough scope. He signaled to me and I reached back for some line to get another turn around the windlass. In my inexperience, I didn't grab enough line and only got a turn around my wrist. Johnny came up through the forward hatch and saw me slip my hand out of the loop just in time. He turned white. I didn't even know how close I had come to losing a hand. After that he taught me that when an anchor line was running out, you had to reach way back and grab as much as possible to safely get a turn on the windlass.

Once the charter started, the work was more demanding. Not only did we have to run and maintain the boat, there was breakfast to fix and serve and a big meal to prepare at the end of the day. I emptied ashtrays, helped to serve drinks on the aft deck and Cap and I both helped with the numerous dishes. I discovered that perfection of service was the norm. If everything was right, there was no comment, but if one little thing was wrong, you'd hear plenty. I got a new perspective on what it was like to be in service. It was a valuable education. After one of these long days, my fold-down pipe berth in the fo'c'sle felt like heaven. Johnny would fall into his bunk below me and always expressed his appreciation in the same way: "Oh boy, oh boy, oh boy, oh boy!" I sure agreed. What, after all, can be better than bed after a long, hard day's work?

One night there was a violent thunderstorm, and we had to get extra lines on the Sears boat under very difficult conditions. I was able to handle the bow lines without being told what to do. After that, Cap began to have a little confidence in me.

When one of Sears' crewmen left, I went on the yawl for one of the races. They gave me very simple things to do. I was amazed at the way Sears cursed his crew. Even more amazing, they all put up with it. When they came aboard *Car-Al II* after the race, they were all good friends again. Such rough usage of the crew must have been customary. On the other hand, maybe the cursing is why his crewman left.

After the charter was over, we did some real yachting on the long, leisurely cruise south.

Car-Al II was a special boat. Lacking many of the amenities and electronics of the modern yacht, she had a simple elegance that most of the modern yachts lack. I take great pride and pleasure in having known her so well.

INDIGO BUNTINGS

Three glowing jewels of indigo,
Their joyful bath begun,
Fling diamond droplets from the stream
Into the morning sun.

COLORADO CHIC

(A Western written by a woman)

Luke had changed his outfit twice. He was going to the square dance at the Governor's home and was determined to make an impression on the Governor's beautiful daughter, Annabelle Preston.

"Shucks, Shorty," Luke said. This shirt don't go with these here chaps worth a hang. I ain't never goin' ter git ready."

"It ain't the shirt, and it ain't the chaps, Luke. Once you strap on that there hand-tooled gun belt yore color coordinatin' will be jest stunnin'. Naw, the problem is yore bandanner. That there mauve don't go with the yaller tobaccer juice stain on yore moustache." Luke shot a stream at the spittoon and wiped his mouth on his sleeve.

"Well, Shorty, this here tobaccer juice blends in right well on this here shirt," he said, looking at his sleeve.

"Tie on this here taupe bandanner," Shorty told him. It'll highlight the yaller stain on yore moustache real purty...."

WATER

A minnow hangs suspended . . .
Transparent, tiny silver shaft of light . . .
Time stops for a perfect instant.

MY DISCOVERY

After some painful minor surgery, I was awake one morning, floating on a sea of painkillers. I turned on my bedside radio and tuned to a station that was playing old standards. Drifting in and out of sleep, I became aware that a female vocalist was singing "In The Wee Small Hours of the Morning." The voice was warm and filled with emotion. The arrangement was perfect . . . caressing, lifting and swirling around the voice like a tropical sea around a beautiful woman. There were tears in my eyes when the song ended. I clenched my fist with frustration when the artist was not identified. I knew I would not be able to contact the station. It was one of those that played music that was programmed on some distant planet. I was right. The station didn't even have a phone number. I could only hope to run across the same artist again and have her identified. Later, I even wondered if my reaction to what I heard had been caused by the music or the painkillers. Months went by and then . . . serendipity struck.

I was exercising on the floor at my gym listening to a talk show on AM radio. I rolled over to do some pushups, accidentally pressed a button on my little radio and changed the station. Suddenly, I was listening to the same version of "In The Wee Small Hours of the Morning." This time they identified the artist: Carly Simon. The Internet took care of the rest.

I found a Carly Simon album called *My Romance*. Sure enough, one of the tracks was "In The Wee Small Hours of the Morning." A week later, I had the album, and I knew for sure that my reaction had not been due to the painkillers.

The whole album is moving, interesting . . . nearly perfect musically. Carly Simon and Marty Paich . . . what a combination!

So many vocalists are just stylists and sound emotionally flat. Ella, Nat King Cole, Cleo Lane and, especially, Tony Bennett all have lots of feeling in their music but, when Carly sings, her interpretations overflow with feeling. She moves with grace from passion to poignancy.

Carly is intensely musical. Her phrasing is lovely, and her voice is unique. Unlike Ella, whose big notes are smooth and bloom into a beautiful tremolo, Carly's big notes are loud and edgy with the slightest tremolo at the end. Her soft notes are warm with a full tremolo. This contrast, the dynamics she uses and the way she slides into a note, combine to create the beauty and interest. Then there is that indefinable something in her voice that makes it more musical than most singers. Call it magic. Ah . . . Carly Simon!

Then there are the arrangements . . . .

I have always loved Marty Paich but knew him more as a jazz arranger. The arrangements he did for Carly's album are something else. Rightly, he puts the emphasis on the piano; and by the way, pianist Michael Kosarin does a wonderful job on this album.

Even when Marty uses the whole orchestra—as in the title song—he is musical and never lets the arrangement sound like an ego pump-up for the singer. His scope is huge, moving from a powerful, irresistible piano in "When Your Lover Has Gone"— that eventually washes over Carly's voice like the tide coming in—to the lightest accents from strings or oboe. He inserts tasty jazz trumpet or sax solos that enhance the feeling of the song. He has the courage to end a song with nothing but the voice or a sustained piano chord, and a couple of pieces do not resolve on the tonic but, like life, leave you floating on what has happened. Ah . . . Marty Paich!

If the sheer beauty and feeling of this album doesn't make you cry, nothing will. It is so far beyond any other vocal album I have ever heard that it is a shame that Carly has nothing else like it. She should record all the great romantic ballads of George Gershwin, Cole Porter, Duke Ellington, Hoagy Carmichael, Irving Berlin and the rest. What a boon to American music it will be, if she does this. What a loss if she doesn't.

My Romance was recorded in 1990. I discovered it in 2001. It makes me wonder what other great music I have missed and how I will ever find it.

MY LITTLE PAINTING*

Iris crown
A verdant slope
That reaches to
The new-plowed fields.
Trees invade the hedgerows.
Then beyond,
I see more green,
Perhaps some pastures . . .
Then a cottage
White against some wooded hills
And distant . . .
Mountains?
Do the clouds deceive?

This tiny window
Draws me out . . .
And out . . .
My soul expands.

---

*My small gem of a landscape painted by Nancy Lloyd.

LET US THINK

I often hear Christians expound on what God wants. It strikes me as presumptuous. How do they know? For that matter, why would a complete and perfect God want anything?

Well, perhaps Christians make their presumptions from reading scripture. But suppose—just suppose—error has crept into the Bible. Maybe back in the musty, dusty past some underfed, fearful tonsured translator—anxious to avoid the rack—succumbed to the Bishop's threats and took out a paragraph here . . . put in a paragraph there. Maybe the Bishop said, "Brother Otto, it would be nice to have a monopoly on this God business. Insert a passage in which Jesus says he is the only way to God."

I don't know if something like this happened or if Jesus really claimed to be the only path to God. I do know, however, that this claim—that excludes so much of mankind—is still very much around. It comes at me at unexpected times.

In the past year I have attended three funerals. At each of these funerals, I was told by the minister or the eulogizer that I must accept Jesus in order to get to heaven.

A funeral is not an appropriate place to proselytize. People come to funerals for closure or to express love, sympathy and support not to be recruited. But the idea that Jesus is the only way to heaven is the lynchpin of evangelical Christianity. And—even at funerals—Christians feel compelled to tell me (in my own best interest, of course) that God will love me and take me into heaven if I accept Jesus as "my personal Lord and Savior."

Doesn't that "if" make God's love conditional? Well, my experience is that conditional love is not love at all. I don't believe that God's love is conditional, so I conclude that this idea of Jesus being the only way to God does not reflect the truth. This is why

A BOX OF TRINKETS

I have such a hard time joining the Christian flock. I have this pernicious habit of thinking.

THE FIRST CHRISTMAS EVE

—An original carol—

Wanderers traveling through the night
Seeking the comfort of shelter and light,
Would no inn or home receive
Wanderers on The First Christmas Eve?

There was a star that appeared in the east
As a sign to man and beast.
Would the eyes that saw believe
The star that shone down on The First Christmas Eve?

Wise men saw and without questioning
Followed the light from afar.
Shepherds in their awe and wonder
Knelt in the light of the star.

Traveling still were the husband and wife
Carrying their sweet burden of life.
Who would their weary need relieve,
Sheltering them on The First Christmas Eve.

Then in a stable in Bethlehem,
A setting so plain for the perfect gem,
The maid lay down her weary head.
Straw from the manger she used for a bed.

There she rested through the night
Waiting to bring the gift of light,
Waiting for the morrow's birth,
That would bring light to all the earth.

A BOX OF TRINKETS

Every hope for every babe and
Each shining star we believe,
Every deed of love and comfort
Honors The First Christmas Eve.

As we go forward through the years,
Filled with hopes and dreams and fears,
Let's look back and all receive
Strength from remembering The First Christmas Eve.

THE FLIMFLAMS

There is a Repository of Mistakes in my brain. It becomes available for viewing at three in the morning.

Three in the morning is a low time. One's metabolism has sunk to its lowest. Physical and mental defenses are weak. It is the hour most people die. It is the hour for viewing . . . mistakes.

I wake around three a.m. for whatever reason—possibly a need to go to the bathroom—and, returning to bed, I compose myself for the remainder of my night's sleep. If I am lucky, I have a book in progress to occupy my mind while I drift back into slumber. Sometimes, if there is something of great interest coming up in my life, I am able to think happy, positive thoughts at three a.m. A new guitar that is soon to arrive will do the trick or an upcoming trip to a beautiful spot. If, however, my mind is without these distractions and my limited skills in meditation fail to give me some blessed nothingness, I usually get invited to view my ROM.

No, no . . . this is not computer memory—though in a sense it is. My "ROM" is my Repository of Mistakes. All my worst mistakes are there. Mistakes that I have long since forgiven and promised to forget are kept bright, shiny and whole in my repository for viewing at three a.m. As I groan and cringe in embarrassment and guilt, they are paraded before my eyes: An old girlfriend seeing me make a fool of myself; unnecessary harshness to a loved one; disloyalty to a friend—mistakes, big and small, old and new—all there for my personal, private viewing. They do not shrink or dim with age. All are fresh and clear dominating my mind with their reality . . . THE FLIMFLAMS!

If I am very lucky, my wife wakes up too.

"I've got the flimflams," I mumble. She understands at once and puts her arms around me saying "there, there" . . . "poor thing" . . . the same words of comfort that were desired by Elwood Dodd's psychiatrist in the movie, *Harvey*. These magical words usually soothe me back to sleep. All too often, however, my wife sleeps on, unaware of my problem. When this happens, there is nothing for it but to get up, have a cup of chamomile tea and read a chapter of Patrick O'Brian. The main characters in the O'Brian novels, Jack Aubrey and Stephen Maturin, are so wonderfully human and so clearly flawed, that I am able to return to my bed drowsy and comforted in the knowledge that I am not alone.

As I write this, I wonder if it may be our flaws that make us human.

I have often noticed that people are more loveable for their mistakes than their successes. Successes can be admired but are more often envied. Mistakes, on the other hand, when they are admitted, draw us into the human fold. Is it possible that we could strengthen our sense of community, if we were more willing to admit and laugh at our own mistakes and weaknesses? Community strengthened by admitting flaws? It's an interesting idea that seems particularly appropriate for us imperfect humans. Perhaps, if I develop this theme and really come to believe in it, it will help me at three in the morning with . . . THE FLIMFLAMS.

THREE WORDS

For me the three most important words in the English language are *home, love,* and *God.* While these words are used in many ways, if you consider them in the sense that makes them important . . . they are all the same thing.

CONNECTED SPRINGS?

Years ago I wrote a poem:

SPRING OF JOY

It gushes forth,
Bubbling,
Sparkling,
Deep and pure,
Reflecting joy . . .
My little boy's laugh.

Later I wrote a poem:

HOWARD SPRING, NOVELIST

Spring, indeed!
A source of pure, clear prose
Flowing from the Cornish countryside,
Reflecting back a pastoral way of life
Threatened by machines and war,
Reflecting English hearts and minds
At their very best.
Refreshment for the thirsty soul.

Yesterday I was thinking what an ideal metaphor "spring" is for an outpouring of something wonderful. When I realized I had used the same metaphor for poems about our little boy, Ben, and a novelist who died decades before Ben was born, I began to wonder if there was a connection between Ben and Howard Spring. Suddenly I realized that without Howard Spring, our little boy would not exist. Therein lies a story.

A BOX OF TRINKETS

I lived in Middlebury, Vermont, for twenty-three years. When I was fifty my wife and I separated and I left Vermont for good.

A couple of years before I left, I had been poking around fruitlessly among thousands of books in an old bookstore. It is almost always fruitless to search at random for a really good novel in an old bookstore. There is just too much junk to wade through. On that particular day, however, I put my hand on a book that was to change the course of my life. The book was called *The Houses In Between* by Howard Spring. Of course, one man's junk is another man's literature, but I make no claims that Spring wrote great literature. All I know is that his writing—the way he expressed his mind—resonated with me. That first novel of his drew me in to such an extent that I didn't stop until I had found all of his novels. Howard Spring became my favorite novelist.

Many of Spring's books are set in Cornwall, England.

After my wife and I separated, I moved to Vero Beach, Florida—probably the worst place on the face of the earth to form a new relationship with a member of the opposite sex. The women around my own age were either married or traumatically divorced . . . "wounded birds." The women who were younger than me looked right through me as if I didn't exist. I discussed this with my wife, with whom I had remained good friends. She suggested that I go to Europe where women had a different attitude. I knew that anything would be an improvement over Vero Beach, but Europe covers a large area. Where to go? I felt sure my possibilities would be enhanced if I shared a common language with whatever women I met, and the Howard Spring novels had made me want to see Cornwall. Several weeks later, I found myself driving through southwest England in a rented car approaching the small Cornish coastal village of St. Mawes.

I checked into a hotel in St. Mawes called The Idle Rocks. Destiny hangs on such slender threads. Had I gotten a decent room in The Idle Rocks, I would not have met my wife-to-be. I was given a room that must have been converted from a storage closet. It was about eight by ten and had no window. When I complained, I was told blandly: "take it or leave it." Without further comment, I picked up my bag and guitar, walked across the street and checked in to The Rising Sun hotel where one Jill Marshall happened to be working as a chambermaid. She was to become the mother of Ben Johnson who, by the way, is destined to become a great storyteller!

The first morning I was in The Rising Sun I returned to my room after breakfast to find a young woman making up my bed. I said I would come back later, but she assured me she was almost finished. She was very smiley and looked at me rather than through me. I pottered around the room while she finished up. Before she left—having seen my Florida address taped to my guitar case—she asked me about Florida, saying that she had a friend there that she might visit.

Evidently I made quite an impression on her as someone who was strange to the point of being an alien from space. I was sitting uncomfortably on the edge of the bed when she asked about Florida, and there was a lamp behind me that was highlighting my large, bald head. I was taken aback to find a young woman who actually saw me. This probably explains the great aplomb with which I told her about Florida: "Uuuh . . . it's . . . uh . . . flat . . . uuuuh . . . and . . .uh . . . purty." What stunning repartee! She later told me that she had never seen anyone quite as peculiar and ill at ease as I was, and she was fascinated!

That day—in order to avoid the stomachache I got driving on the Cornish roads—I took the ferry from St. Mawes to Falmouth to visit Howard Spring's home. It was a successful trip that involved a long, scenic walk through Falmouth to Spring's home. There was a caretaker there who kindly took me inside and showed me the desk where Spring had written many of his novels. I remember that on the way back to the ferry I stopped in a small restaurant for a cream tea.

The next morning I bumped into Jill Marshall in the corridor outside my room. I had myself a bit more together. I gave her my card and said that if she got to Florida, she would be welcome to visit. She thanked me warmly and suggested that perhaps we could become pen pals, so I gave her another card on which she wrote her address. She said that she wrote about thirty letters a week but that very few people wrote back. I looked her right in the eye and said firmly, "I'll write."

I wrote the next day from another Cornish hotel further up the coast. She, too, wrote the next day.

Back in Florida, our correspondence flourished and the letters got longer. Eight pages, twelve pages, eighteen pages! Finally I called her. It messed up the letter writing, but I couldn't resist. The calls got longer. Fifteen minutes, a half an hour an hour, two hours! Finally I said, "I can't stand this any longer. You've got to come over."

"What," she said, "as a kind of pet?"

"No," I replied, "as a wife."

I sent her a dozen roses and that tipped the balance. She agreed to come. She never went back!

Ours was definitely an unconventional courtship. Our wedding was equally unconventional being on a small boat with a golden retriever as matron of honor!

So is there a connection between Howard Spring and Ben? Well they are both wonderful storytellers . . . and, as I remarked above, without Howard Spring, our son Ben would not exist. Is this simply a grand coincidence, or is there another question to ask? Doesn't "spring" as a metaphor for an outpouring of beauty or joy imply the question: what is the source of such outpourings? If the source is God, couldn't the source of all "springs" be a common source? This indeed would be a connection!

CONTINUUM

Mythology's
The past that never was.

Science fiction is
The future that will never be.

Man is in between
Creating both.

THE LADY IN RED
A Ghost Story

There were no brass bands when Sergeant Wilson Prescott came back from war . . . not that I wanted any. All I wanted was to go home.

The Prescotts have had a plantation since the late seventeen hundreds. It's called "Lebanon" named after the small Mississippi town on the Yazoo River in Holmes County. There wasn't much left of Lebanon Plantation . . . several hundred acres of Mississippi cotton land out of what used to be thousands and a plantation house that was covered with vines. The house—situated near the riverbank—was rotting and falling in on itself. I didn't care about that. Since my parents were both dead, I knew the old house would provide the solitude I craved. At Lebanon there were only two old family retainers . . . an aging black couple called Jobie and Bole Weevil. I can't help it. That's what he was called.

The bus dropped me in Cruger and I got a ride with a farmer out the Old Lebanon Road to the plantation. I was going to hide there and write about the war. I had no ambitions to write the great American war novel. I just felt that if I wrote about the war I might stop having nightmares about shooting children who were trying to kill me. My body had been lucky in Vietnam. I had received only minor wounds—a peppering of shrapnel from a mortar round. My mind hadn't done so well. It wasn't what I had seen that gave me the nightmares; it was what I had done.

The old house looked just the same, only slightly more rotted. After I had said hello to Bole Weevil and Jobie, and finally stopped her from clucking over me, I changed from my uniform into some old slacks, a tee shirt and some loafers. I looked in the mirror. It didn't look like me. I looked like someone I used to know.

Downstairs, I found Jobie had made a nice lunch.

"I done made all yo' favorites, Mr. Will," she said.

I thanked her. She had given me fried chicken, rice and greens, but I couldn't eat much. I pushed my food around on the plate while Jobie stood by looking more worried than ever. After a chicken leg and a glass of milk, I pushed back from the table and went to the library where I sat down at the old typewriter I had used in college. Nothing came to me. I sat there and looked at my hands . . . made green by the light flooding in through the vines that had overgrown the tall windows and French doors of the library. I was tired to the bone. Finally I stumbled over to the old horsehair sofa and fell out. I slept like a dead man.

. . . A firefight was going on. We had called in an air strike on the village at the edge of the jungle. Sniper fire from there had killed two guys in my squad. The fighter-bomber screamed in and napalm rolled—in orange-black fury—over the village. A young girl ran flaming from the village screaming. A burst from my M-16 stopped her screaming . . . I woke and sat up, tears streaming down my face. It was my first nightmare back at the plantation. . . . Welcome home.

Three months later after writing two hundred and eighty pages, the nightmares were worse. It was the third day of August.

That day I stopped writing around noon and came out of the library for lunch. Jobie was still giving me good meals and clucking over me like chicken.

"You got to eat, Mr. Will. You skin and bones," she fussed.

"Leave me alone, Jobie," I told her absently for the three-hundredth time.

I had caught a glimpse of myself in the yellowed mirror in the hall. I was thin. I didn't care. I managed to swallow something, left the table, went back in the library and locked myself in. I sat for hours trying to write, but I couldn't get started again. My theory about writing myself out of the nightmares hadn't held up. I knew the writing was making everything worse. There was no point in going on with it. I looked at my shotgun in the gun case between the bookshelves. I couldn't pull my eyes away. More and more grayness filled my mind. What I had written had no meaning. Life had no meaning. Only the shotgun had meaning. It was a way out. I tore my eyes away from the gun case and stumbled out of the library. There was a bottle of bourbon in the butler's pantry. I took it to the front porch and sat in the twilight with the bottle. Jobie and Bole Weevil had gone home. I was alone. I sat on the front porch drinking and trying not to think about the shotgun. I saw the lights of a car coming up the long gravel drive. It pulled up near the steps where I sat. The driver got out leaving the lights on. A redheaded young woman with freckles got out with a glass-covered dish. I was partly dazzled by the headlights and didn't recognize her.

"Wilson?" she said.

"Yeah," I answered. "Who's that?" I must have looked pretty bad. I hadn't bathed, shaved or changed clothes for days. I had lost weight. I had drunk half a fifth of bourbon.

"It's me, Jan Harris." The Harris place was next to Lebanon Plantation just up the river. She moved out of the glare and I could see her.

"You grew up," I said. She was looking at me like she couldn't believe her eyes.

"What happened to you, Wilson?"

"Vietnam," I told her.

"You're drunk," she said.

"Yeah, I am," I admitted.

"Momma sent me over with a casserole." She extended the dish.

"I don't want it," I told her rudely. She looked at me for a minute. Biting her lip and shaking her head once in puzzlement, she got back in her car and drove away.

That night I woke after another bad dream. I lay in bed sweating. The frogs and cicadas had quit and the night was still. The moon was about to set. I sat up remembering the shotgun downstairs. It drew me with a magnetic attraction. My sweat was drying. It was hot but I began to feel chilled.

"Help me," I sat me up with surprise. It was a woman's whisper coming from outside.

"Who's there?" I said, going to the window.

"Help me, Jason. I'm caught." I felt my way down the stairs not turning on any lights. I went out the back door and moved across the overgrown lawn and into the oak trees. I felt Spanish moss brush my face. I moved quietly as I had learned to move through the jungle in Vietnam.

"Jason . . ." I heard the whisper again, near the river. I saw a redness near the bank of the river. It was a light without light . . . a transparent redness that illuminated nothing. As I approached I saw a whiteness that seemed to be a woman's face and the redness took on the form of a dress. What appeared to be black hair streamed across her neck and shoulders . . . coils of blackness in the strange light. She turned her face to me. Except for the eyes, it was beautiful. The eyes were completely white and dead looking. A shiver prickled up my spine, but I forced myself to go closer.

"Release me, Jason."

As I approached I saw her better. She wore long white gloves. I saw that her hair was dark auburn, not black. On dainty feet she wore black boots. I reached towards the image and it faded . . . disappeared. I must have stood there for five minutes feeling numb. Finally the coldness faded and I rubbed my eyes . . . wondering if it was the booze or if I was going over the brink mentally. For some reason, before I returned to the house, I reached up for a dead limb and broke it off. I stuck it into the soft, black earth marking the spot where I had been standing.

The next morning I popped awake with a question ringing in my mind, "Who was Jason?"

It was Jobie's day off. After I made toast and coffee, I went to the library to the oak filing cabinets where family papers were stored. My grandmother had been a genealogy fanatic and had kept well-organized family records dating back to the early eighteen hundreds. On the way to the library, I caught a whiff of myself.

"Ye Gods!" I said out loud. "Just because I'm a wreck is no reason I have to smell like one." After a shower and shave and some clean clothes, I looked—and smelled—better. Had I not been so gaunt, I would have been presentable . . . not that I had anyone to be presented to. Then I thought of Jan Harris. I decided to walk over and apologize to her and her mother. But first . . . the library.

As I entered I looked at the gun case. Something had changed. The gun was there but now it was just a gun. It no longer had any power to dominate my thoughts. I wondered why. Then I realized that what I had seen last night had—for the first time since Vietnam—made me interested in something besides myself.

"Well, if I'm going crazy," I said out loud, "at least it's an interesting way to go."

I took out the file that said "Family Tree" and began to flip through, scanning for a Jason. I found him on the fourth page: Jason Prescott, 1803–1833. The chronological files went back to 1830, so I thought I had a chance of finding something about him.

The file from 1830–1840 was thin. There were a few letters but none mentioned Jason Prescott. There were records of crops and one record of slave births and deaths and a badly yellowed clipping from a newspaper. The masthead was missing but the date was there. I read:

> SUICIDE MAY BE MURDER/SUICIDE
> The body of Jason Prescott—an apparent suicide—was found in his bedroom by his manservant today. Further foul play is feared.
>
> Mr. Prescott's fiancée, Barbara Landry—the daughter of the owners of the Landry Plantation near Egypt, Mississippi—is missing and feared murdered. Under close questioning by the Sheriff, Miss Grace Landry, sister of the missing young woman, admitted that her sister was with child. It is feared that Prescott discovered this fact, killed his fiancée and committed suicide. A massive search is underway around the Prescott Plantation, but so far there is no trace of the missing woman.
>
> The Prescott house servants told of their master—in a rage with a shotgun— chasing them from the house, thus leaving Prescott alone for some time with his fiancée.
>
> Miss Landry is five feet three inches tall and has long auburn hair. When last seen she was wearing a red dress, white gloves and black boots. Any person having information about a woman fitting this description should contact Holmes County Sheriff, Joseph Heatherton immediately.

The date of the article was August 3, 1833! Last night had been the anniversary of the death of Barbara Landry! I had to tell someone about this. It was all too amazing. I remembered the calm, steady gaze of Jan Harris and my desire to apologize. In my withdrawal from the world, I had not bothered to acquire a car, but it was only a twenty-minute walk to the Harris place. I put the fragile article in an envelope and left the house.

"So you don't think I'm crazy?" I asked Jan after I had finished telling her the story. Jan slid the article back in the envelope.

"Not now," she replied. "I did the night I brought the casserole over . . . crazy and drunk. Wilson, I want to see the place where you saw this vision."

"I think I can find it," I told her. "I stuck a dead branch in the ground to mark the spot."

"Why did you do that?" she asked, looking at me intently.

"I don't know," I said truthfully. "I just did."

We found the dead branch.

"The vision was right over there by the river bank," I pointed. We went to the place. There was a slight depression in the ground—about five feet long and three feet wide. We looked at each other.

"A grave . . ." she said.

"I'll get a shovel," I replied.

It didn't take long to remove the soft, black dirt. The shovel hit something hard. I got on my hands and knees in the hole. It was about three feet deep. I swept dirt from a flat smooth surface. A slab of glass began to appear. I brushed more dirt away and leaned closer to examine the glass.

"Jesus!" I screamed, jumping backwards in the grave. "Jesus, God Almighty!"

There, beneath the glass, floated the dead white face of a beautiful girl with auburn hair swirling about her head. Only the eyes were ghastly and blank. They were even whiter than the face.

After I had calmed down, we excavated around the glass-topped iron coffin. The rest of the girl came into view. She was floating in some kind of clear liquid. Red dress, black boots, white gloves . . . all were perfect. Only the eyes were wrong.

Let's open it," I said. I went to the tool shed for a crowbar. It took our combined weight to lever up the iron frame that held the glass. We were assaulted by a powerful smell of alcohol.

"It smells like pure grain alcohol," I said.

"Where in the world would Jason Prescott find that much alcohol?" she said, "not to mention a glass-topped iron coffin."

"Maybe he didn't kill her in a rage," I replied. "Maybe he found out beforehand and had time to plan the murder."

"If that's what happened," she said, "he must have been insane."

The perfectly preserved skin of the corpse was already starting to discolor where the air had touched it.

"What now?" Jan wanted to know.

"A cremation," I said. "I want to release some ghosts."

I went to the house and came back with some matches and my manuscript. I fanned it out in my hand and lit the edge of the paper. As the pages caught, I placed the flaming manuscript carefully in the coffin.

"Your ghosts, too?" she asked taking my hand.

Not wanting to see the beautiful face distort from the fire, we backed away from the coffin. Blue flame spread over the alcohol.

"Yes. They'll just be bad memories, now," I said. "They won't haunt me any longer."

We smiled into each other's eyes as blue fire spiraled into the Mississippi twilight.

Note: This story has a basis in fact. In *Mississippi Off the Beaten Path* by Marlo Carter Kirkpatrick, there is a factual account of the discovery of a perfectly preserved body of a young woman with auburn hair who was dressed in a red velvet dress. The body had been preserved in alcohol in a cast-iron coffin with a glass lid. The coffin was unearthed in 1969 on the Egypt plantation in Holmes County, Mississippi. Thanks to our dear friend, Father Benjamin Bell, for sending me the factual story and suggesting that I write a short story about The Lady in Red.

DID JESUS LAUGH?

There is a very well-written and beautifully produced New Age magazine called *IONS* published by the Institute of Noetic Sciences. The following excerpt of a letter that I wrote to *IONS* is self-explanatory:

Dear Editors,

I received the recent issue of *IONS* and found it very interesting. . . .

One thing troubled me about the magazine, however: I searched in it in vain for a trace of humor. It makes me wonder if you are becoming religious—that is, taking yourself too seriously. The Bible, for example, is totally without humor.

There is no reference in the gospels to Jesus laughing. Jesus was supposed to have been fully human. If so, he would have laughed. What is more human than laughter?

My belief is that when priests or holy men translate sacred texts they expunge what they don't like. It is possible that early translators feared humor might prevent scripture from being taken seriously. For this reason, they may have removed all traces of humor.

I'll bet you that God loves humor and fun.

I read one time that God should be approached playfully. Several days after I read this, I was resting and thought: "Hey, God. Do you want to come out and play?" At once my mind was flooded with joy and an amazing pattern of woven bands of light. I call what I saw "the warp and woof of God."

Anyway, my complaint about the New Age movement has been that it takes itself too seriously. Therefore let me contribute a bit of humor that you can print just for the fun of it! It's a short poem.

HEADLINES OF TWO MIRACLES

Spontaneous Remission Inoperable Tumor

New Ager Found With Sense of Humor.

With warm regards and thanks for a good magazine,

Allen Johnson, Jr.
Web site: www.allenjohnsonjr.com
E-mail: allen@allenjohnsonjr.com

    This letter raises a couple of questions that people don't usually ask:
    Did Jesus laugh?
    Is fun and humor compatible with spirituality?
    What is even more interesting to me than these questions, however, is the response that my letter elicited. After the letter was published, e-mails came pouring in. One was from two Bible scholars . . . a long, rather defensive letter that gave me numerous examples of humor in the Bible. Most of the examples were far-fetched. Even so, their letter taught me that I shouldn't make absolute statements like, "The Bible . . . is totally without humor."
    All the other e-mails were in agreement with what I had written. Writers expressed their agreement with considerable feeling. One writer said that when he read my letter, he broke down and wept! Clearly, my letter had raised some questions that many others had been asking—questions that had touched the feelings of quite a number of people. The reaction my letter got makes me believe that the question of humor and spirituality is one that should be explored even if the exploration only leads to more questions.
    For example, since humor is so human, wouldn't it be easier to relate to Jesus if we had at least one example of him laughing?

OPPOSING MIRRORS

As I put this collection together, it occurs to me that often I am writing about my own writing. I suppose this could be seen as self-absorption which, if carried too far, would be like the bird who flew in ever-diminishing circles until it flew up its own . . . er . . . bottom. Or, it could be seen as similar to looking in opposing mirrors where the vista is one of ever diminishing clarity!

I may be writing about my writing, because I have gotten in the habit of trying—on author school visits—to explain to thousands of children how and why I write. I try to explain to them how my writing is connected to my life . . . how what I have done and what I have thought has influenced what I write. Children are interested in this connectedness. Perhaps the readers of this collection will be interested too.

On the other hand, with this piece I am writing about my writing about my writing . . .

Whoops! Opposing mirrors!

BOVINE SUFFRAGE

If cows had the vote,
It is certainly true
That all politicians
Would learn how to moo.

But then all the polls
Would be lacking in couth,
'Cause bovine hindquarters
Won't fit in the booth.

And like politicians,
The polls would be full
Of that good bovine stuff
We abbreviate "bull"!

FIBBER MCGEE AND MOLLY

When I was a boy in the 1940s, there was no television. We listened to radio for entertainment and many of the shows were delightful. Back in the Nineties I bought some tapes of some of the shows I used to listen to and found many of them just as much fun as I remembered them. One disappointment was "The Jack Benny Show."

Jack Benny had a giant comic talent and a strong, easily recognized personality and voice. He was the ideal radio comedian. Unfortunately, the show relied too heavily on Jack Benny. It was badly written. It was so badly written that I gave away all of the Jack Benny tapes that I bought. "Fibber McGee and Molly" was different. It was a well-written show and stood the test of time.

In the Fifties, American pop culture became insipid. After swing and before rock-and-roll, popular music was mostly gooey, simplistic ballads and idiotic novelty tunes. Insipid sitcoms like "The Donna Reed Show" also sowed the seeds for the rebellion of the Sixties. Radio sitcoms of the Forties, however, were wholesome without being insipid. Their humor came from the flaws, foibles and mistakes of the characters. "Fibber McGee and Molly" was a good example.

Deeply incompetent yet irrepressibly confident in his abilities, McGee was always getting in over his head. Patient, tolerant Molly was the perfect foil for her husband.

McGee—in an attempt to fit the front door on the coldest day of winter—might cut the door off six inches too short. He might catch Old Muley—the biggest bass in Dugan's lake—one day before the season opened. No matter. Molly's exasperation never overcame her tolerance. Somehow McGee would, at the last minute, always manage to pull the fat from the fire.

Many of the characters and jokes were "regulars" on the show. You could count on them to appear nearly every week.

McGee had a hall closet that was so crammed with junk that, if someone mistakenly opened the door, everything would fall out with an extended crashing, banging and tinkling that was a sound-effects man's dream. This joke happened almost every week and was always funny. Far from being boring, the repetitions created continuity and a familiarity that made you feel right at home with the McGees. This joke was so well known that it found its way into the language for a time. Any ungodly household mess was called "McGee's closet."

There was another humorous bit that got into the language. The McGees had a friend, a timid, henpecked little man called Mr. Wimple. Every time "Wimp" appeared on the show he would relate some awful story of abuse from his huge, bullying wife, "Sweetieface." I am sure Mr. Wimple helped the term "wimp" to become a permanent part of the language.

Another situation joke that was always funny happened with Mayor LaTrivia. The McGees would deliberately misunderstand the mayor and stick with the misunderstanding until LaTrivia was totally exasperated and confused.

These repeated humorous situations were written and performed with such skill that they never became tired. Since you knew exactly what was going to happen, you felt included.

The show was spiced up by a very good swing band called The Billy Mills Orchestra. Alas, there was a vocal group called The Kings Men that even the stunning guitar accompaniment of George Van Eps could not save from being corny.

Underneath all the confusion, irritation and mistakes in these shows is the unspoken feeling that all the characters care deeply about each other. In fact, it is their mistakes that make the characters so human and lovable. The listener is drawn in to a sense of community that is so strong that it feels like being in a big family.

Our little boy, Ben, listens with me to old radio tapes before going to sleep. I love the continuity of his growing up with some of the same warm, funny influences I knew as a boy.

As we listen, the doorbell rings. It's Mayor LaTrivia. Ben grins at me. He knows exactly what is going to happen!

YOUNG MEN ON FIRE!

Benny
Cool clarinet-fire
Pouring . . . soaring . . .

Harry
Hot trumpet-fire
Flashing . . . flaming . . .

Gene
Pulsing drum-fire
Pushing . . . driving . . .

Jess
Sweet piano-fire
Striding . . . swinging . . .

Young men on fire!

MY WINNIE THE POOH TEA MUGS

My English mother-in-law gave us some white porcelain tea mugs with Ernest H. Shepard Winnie The Pooh illustrations on their surfaces. For some reason every time I reach for one of these mugs, my heart lifts. I always wonder why I get a little burst of joy from these mugs. I was not exposed to Winnie The Pooh as a child and only recently—reading to my little boy—discovered the charm of the Pooh stories. Often a possession will cause a happy feeling from time to time but the Pooh mugs are different. They lift my heart every time I use them.

I believe it has to do with the Shepard illustrations. Something about the simple, sunny, innocence of these colorful little pictures slips past my adult mind and gives me the joy of seeing once more as a child.

Ernest H. Shepard, who also did wonderful illustrations for *The Wind in the Willows*, saw things as a child, and with his talent he was able help other adults to see as a child. What a wonderful gift to pass on to the world.

BOTHER AND O BLOW!*

(My favorite poem from my book *A Breeze in the Willows.*)

When a mole must do spring cleaning,
He will work quite hard and so,
Moley shocked himself by saying,
"Bother and O Blow!"

But his heart was filled with longing,
And his molish will was rent
By the soft insistent calling
Of spring's sweet discontent.

So the Mole said: "Hang spring cleaning!"
And he bolted from his home,
And he scratched and scrooged and scrabbled
Up through the fragrant loam.

And his snout popped into sunlight,
And thus it came to pass
That a Mole did roll in pure delight
In the warm, sweet meadow grass.

---

*Reprinted with permission from *A Breeze in the Willows* by Allen Johnson, Jr. Copyright 1997 by Allen Johnson, Jr., Ten Speed Press, Berkeley, CA. Available from your local bookseller, by calling 800-841-2665, or by visiting www.tenspeed.com

FOUR EXTRAORDINARY WOMEN I NEVER KNEW

The Beauty

I was watching live television coverage of an outdoor jazz festival. The camera zoomed in on a young woman in a blue dress. She had shining, medium-length black hair that swept up in a natural curl at the end.

This young woman was covered with freckles. You could see hints of white skin between the freckles but, for the most part, her skin was a sea of brown freckles. "Poor thing," I thought until I looked closer. She was the most beautiful woman I had ever seen. The camera zoomed in on her face. She had startling, dark-blue eyes. For some reason I am yet to understand, her freckles—more than I had ever seen on anyone—enhanced her breathtaking beauty. The camera moved. I have never forgotten her.

The Lover

Sadly, the term "lover" has come to mean a sexual relationship outside of marriage. This is not what I mean by the young woman who came to the pool where I was swimming laps. I, and a frail man—even older than me—were resting between laps. A young woman in a bathing suit—a slender, attractive, brunette, possibly nineteen or twenty—squatted down next to the old man, smiled at him and spoke briefly. I didn't hear what she said but the warmth of her smile spoke volumes. It said,

"I am twenty and you are eighty and you are my brother. I love you because I know that inside we are the same."

He could have been her grandfather, but he wasn't. I saw her bestow the same loving warmth on two old ladies who were waiting for an exercise class to start. I wondered how such humanity had found its way into one so young.

The Otter

Swimming is boring. To makes the laps pass faster, I watch people under water. An attractive young woman in a bikini in the next lane can make thirty laps seem like fifteen. My wife and I both believe that people can feel your gaze. Once, in the pool, a woman gave me a dirty look, got out and changed lanes!

The really strong swimmers attack the water—legs striking the surface like bricks dropped from fifteen feet . . . arms slapping the water . . . lots of energy expended.

One day I was watching a young woman who was two lanes over. Her body was liquid motion conforming in graceful curves to every current and swirl of the water. She moved through the water with no splash or wasted energy. She was a part of it. We both stopped to rest at the same time.

"You swim like an otter," I said.

"Thank you," she said. "You're not so bad yourself."

It was true. As a swimmer, I was "not so bad" but she . . . ah, she . . . was an otter!

The Smiler

She was about to get into the car. A young man held the door for her. As she bent to get into the car she looked up at the young man and smiled. I have never seen such a radiant face. The smile compounded her natural beauty a hundredfold. It spoke of love and great inner light. It was a stunning vision that lasted only a moment. I feel sure that my mind translated this powerful moment of beauty into something that does not exist: perfection.

THE APOLOGY

I was in the Birmingham Municipal Auditorium with five thousand other Nat King Cole fans listening to the master sing. It was early in the performance. I was sitting just to the left of the center aisle. I heard the thump, thump, thump of running feet and, in the dim light, saw shadowy figures crouched over running towards the stage. "Fans," I thought, "running up for a better look."

Security was tight. There were five or six burly policemen on either side of the stage. The front of the stage was protected by a wide orchestra pit. When the running figures reached the orchestra pit, they jumped it, caught the edge of the stage and pulled themselves up. One dived for Nat King Cole's legs. Cole went down. The police quickly moved in from the wings. Then, as if we were Romans watching gladiators, five thousand people watched a pitched battle on the stage: heads split by nightsticks, teeth flying, blood spattering . . . The thugs were quickly subdued, and Cole was helped from the stage. Thousands of women started to cry. Thousands of men took off their jackets wanting to fight. The police took the thugs away. There was no one to fight. The crowd, on its feet, started to clap. A standing ovation went on and on for five to ten minutes. Finally, Cole's manager came on stage, and the applause died away.

"Mr. Cole would come back out," he said, "but he thinks he may have hurt his back, and he wants to go to the hospital to have it checked out."

A voice from the audience—near the stage—called out what we all felt,

"Just tell him we're sorry!"

The ovation started again and continued for a long time.

Poor Birmingham really didn't need another stain from racial hatred.

When this event has been reported, the emphasis has always been put on the violence and hatred behind the attack. But this was from just a few thugs.

I choose to focus on the massive outpouring of love and admiration behind the apology.

ROMANCE ON I-65

Expressway travel, like plane travel, is a non-experience . . . hours of boredom with the ever-present possibility of sudden death.

Traveling south on I-65, from Birmingham to Pensacola, there is an amusing sign with a likeness of the devil that says: "Go to church or the devil will get you!" My wife and I can chuckle over this for a few miles; then monotony reasserts itself. There are, however, some interesting green road signs—each with the names of two upcoming towns. Four of these double-name signs (TYSON/MONTGOMERY, GEORGIANA/STARLINGTON, JEMISON/THORSBY and GRACE/GARLAND) inspired my wife and me to compose this sultry yet tender . . . taut but smoldering, antebellum romance.

GEORGIANA STARLINGTON, clad in her petticoat, pouted in front of her full-length mirror. She had been holding her cascading auburn curls away from her neck while powdering her already perfect creamy shoulders. She spoke to her cousin, GRACE GARLAND.

"Ah do so hate it when it's sticky! Grace, darlin', how am I to look cool and fresh for the ball tonight? Ah know my silk dress (seeulk drayus) will simply wilt (weeult) in this heat!"

Grace—lovely in her own right, with olive skin and dark brown hair framing her small, oval face—cast a cynical, brown-eyed glance at her beautiful cousin.

"Georgiana, you have everything (evruhthing)—beauty, love . . . everything—and still you're never (nevuh) satisfied. Do you think for a minute that TYSON MONTGOMERY will care if your silk dress is a little limp (leeump)?"

Georgiana had, in fact, just been imagining Tyson, her tall, hawk-like Confederate captain, resplendent in his gray uniform. She had been seeing herself sweeping down the long, curving staircase to greet him while the light of a hundred candles caused her green silk gown and auburn curls to twinkle with jewel-like fires.

Grace would have been more patient, but her cousin's pouting remark had interrupted her own reverie. Reclining on the chaise in her petticoat, she had been dreaming of JEMISON THORSBY, the tall, black-haired young doctor who was visiting from Savannah. Grace had met Jemison only two days ago, but his eyes had locked onto hers with a dark intensity that made her catch her breath with a little gasp....

I would tell you more about how the lives of these four young people were entwined—only to be driven asunder by the war—but the Evergreen exit is coming up, and it's time for turnip greens and fried chicken at the Quality Inn!

Printed in the United States
781500002B